Francis Bacon Portraits and Heads

Francis Bacon

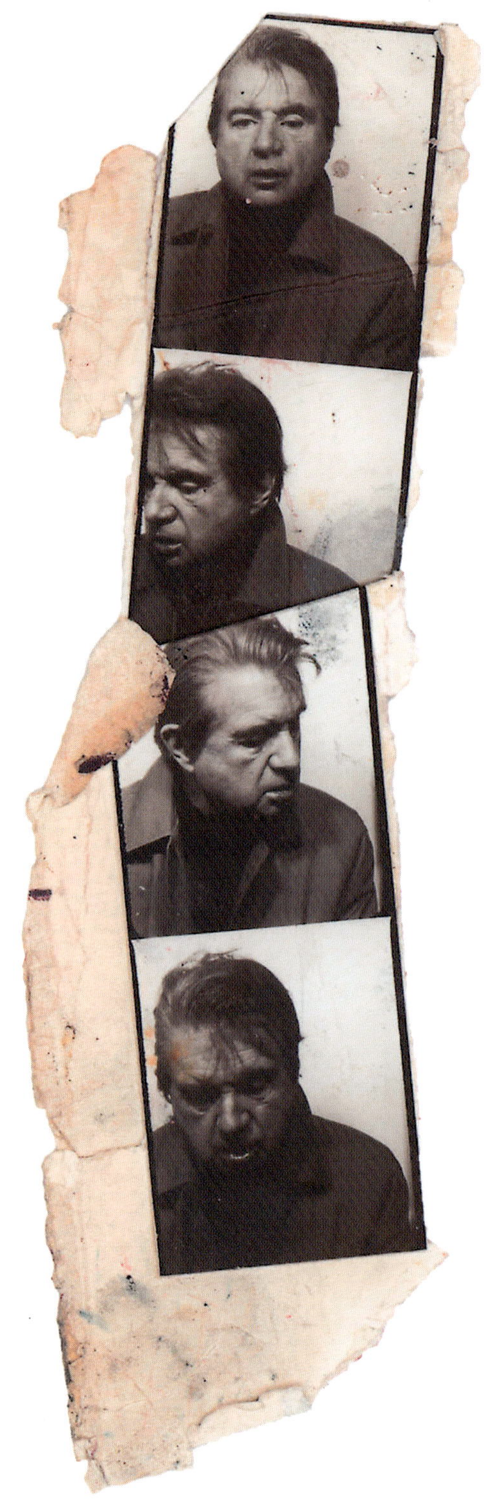

Portraits and Heads

NATIONAL GALLERIES OF SCOTLAND *in association with the* BRITISH COUNCIL

Foreword

This exhibition was conceived and originally selected two years ago by the British Council. I am very grateful to Andrea Rose, Director of Visual Arts, British Council, for proposing it to us, marking as it does the tenth anniversary of the successful partnership between our two institutions on *From London*. This was an exhibition of six post-war figurative painters, the most senior of whom was Francis Bacon. I would also like to acknowledge the financial contribution that the British Council has made towards the transport costs of the present exhibition.

Francis Bacon: Portraits and Heads has been developed and expanded in close collaboration with Richard Calvocoressi, Director of the Scottish National Gallery of Modern Art, and Philip Long, senior curator at the Gallery. I would like to thank them both for their substantial work on the organisation of the show and the catalogue. We are delighted that the Hamburg Kunsthalle will be showing the exhibition in a somewhat different version after Edinburgh as the last before retirement of its distinguished director, Uwe M. Schneede. Christoph Heinrich, chief curator of contemporary art at the Hamburg Kunsthalle, has been involved in the formulation of the exhibition from an early stage and has negotiated important loans.

Competition for loans of Bacon's pictures has become increasingly intense in the years since the artist's death and we would like to acknowledge and thank the many public collections and foundations which have generously agreed to lend to this exhibition, including the Staatliche Museen zu Berlin, Nationalgalerie; Museum Bochum; Museum of Contemporary Art, Chicago; Dublin City Gallery The Hugh Lane; Kunstsammlung Nordrhein-Westfalen, Düsseldorf; Arts Council Collection, England; Hamburg Kunsthalle; Louisiana Museum of Modern Art, Humlebaek; Tate, London; Museo Thyssen-Bornemisza, Madrid; The Whitworth Art Gallery, The University of Manchester; Walker Art Center, Minneapolis; Yale Center for British Art, New Haven; The Metropolitan Museum of Art, New York; The Museum of Modern Art, New York; Musée National d'Art Moderne, Centre Georges Pompidou, Paris; Moderna Museet, Stockholm; Tehran Museum of Contemporary Art; Museum Moderner Kunst, Stiftung Ludwig, Vienna; National Museums and Galleries of Wales; and the Yageo Foundation. We are also indebted to the numerous private collectors who have so generously lent works, including Mr Richard S. Zeisler, Mr and Mrs J. Tomilson Hill, and the many other lenders who wish to remain anonymous.

I would also like to thank the following who have generously helped towards the preparation of the exhibition and catalogue in various ways: Kate Austin, Ernst Beyeler, Ivor Braka, Margarita Cappock, Melanie Clore, Claire Cullen, Barbara Dawson, Thomas Dane, Gerard Faggionato, Lucian Freud, Martin Harrison, Andras Kalman, Andrew Kalman,

Alexander Kearney, Gwendoline Keywood, Julie Lee-Amies, Samantha Lewis, Tomàs Llorens, Glenn D. Lowry, Lars Nittve, Hiroko Onoda, Pilar Ordovás, Francis Outred, Geoffrey Parton, Anna Pryer, Alireza Sami-Azar, Sabine Rewald, Angela Schneider, Tony Shafrazi, Timothy Taylor, Christoph Vitali and Jane Willoughby de Eresby. We would also like to extend our warm thanks to Martin Hammer, senior lecturer in art history at the University of Edinburgh, for his illuminating essay, and to Brian Clarke and Elizabeth Beatty of the Bacon Estate for their support of the exhibition from its inception and for their advice throughout its development. Finally, Andrea Rose would like to extend her thanks to Frank Auerbach, Michael Bird, Emily Butler, Diana Eccles, Kate Eustace, William Feaver, Massimo Martino, Sandy Nairne, and Kathleen Soriano; and to Michael Willson and Nazgol Reypour of the British Council, Iran, for negotiating the loan of a Bacon painting from Tehran, not seen in Britain since 1967.

In Edinburgh the exhibition has been sponsored by Lloyds TSB Scotland and supported by Bentley Edinburgh, as part of the Scottish National Gallery of Modern Art's *Icons of the 20th Century* series, taking place in 2005. We are very grateful to them both.

SIR TIMOTHY CLIFFORD
Director-General, National Galleries of Scotland

After the success of the exhibition, *Andy Warhol: Self-Portraits*, we are delighted to continue our sponsorship of the series, *Icons of the 20th Century*. The exhibition, *Francis Bacon: Portraits and Heads* is another powerful and stimulating show, which is sure to draw in the crowds.

We are very proud of our highly successful partnership with the National Galleries of Scotland, which spans four years, and which has helped to bring many major works of art to Scotland for an increasing number of visitors to enjoy.

This exhibition is no exception, bringing together important works from galleries and private collections all over the world, and helping to cement Scotland's reputation as a thriving centre for the arts.

SUSAN RICE
Chief Executive, Lloyds TSB Scotland

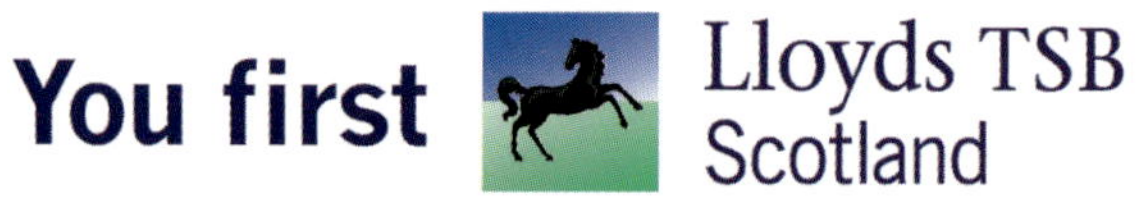

Introduction

This is the first museum exhibition ever devoted to Francis Bacon's portraits – mostly small heads and related full-length figures. To some extent, they tell the story of Bacon's involvement with certain individuals – with lovers such as Peter Lacy and George Dyer; with fellow painters such as Lucian Freud and Frank Auerbach; with drinking companions such as Muriel Belcher, Isabel Rawsthorne and Henrietta Moraes; and with friends such as Bruce Bernard, the photo-historian; John Hewitt, a renowned dealer in antiquities and ethnographic art; and the French writer and philosopher Michel Leiris. They also form a biography of the artist himself, from the early heads painted with dash and verve, to the portraits at the end of his life: faint, spectral, verging on the sentimental. When asked why he began painting his long series of self-portraits, he answered characteristically, 'I couldn't think what on earth to do next, so I thought, "why not try and do myself?"'

To a greater extent, though, the exhibition is about Bacon's singular achievement in defining what portraiture could be. Many of the portraits are not portraits at all in the sense of one person sitting for another to have a likeness taken. Works in the exhibition, dating from the late 1940s, are not even of individuals. They are composites put together from photographs and memory. What they do have is an astonishing ability to seize the instant, to get down in paint not only the surprise and immediacy of the moment, but to sustain it. Bacon was intensely aware of how difficult this was to do. 'I'm not a preacher. I've nothing to say about "the human condition." What gives the pictures their desperate look, if they have one, is the technical difficulty of making appearances at the present stage of the evolution of painting. If my people look as if they're in a dreadful fix, it's because I can't get them out of a technical dilemma.'

Bacon spelled out the dilemma in a tribute written for Matthew Smith's exhibition at the Tate Gallery in 1953: 'Matthew Smith seems to me to be one of the very few English painters since Constable and Turner to be concerned with painting – that is, with making the idea and technique inseparable. Painting in this sense tends towards a complete interlocking of image and paint, so that the image is the paint and vice versa. Here the brush-stroke creates the form and does not merely fill it in.' In the portraits selected for this exhibition, particularly in the small heads (where the heads are in fact the same size as in the larger paintings, but there is no framing device, no surrounding, nothing to interrupt the focus on the head itself), Bacon coaxes, drags, whips and sometimes flogs the paint into shape. The image that emerges is indistinguish-able from the paint that created it, just as the present is indivisible from the past. In the essays that follow, mention is made of the photographic sources found in Bacon's studio after his death. Like many of the greatest painters, however, Bacon strove to integrate instantaneity with what is enduring, holding ancient and modern in balance. If he used photographs and film stills as his starting point, painting ultimately triumphed only if, as he put it: 'you were able to take advantage of what happens when you splash the stuff down'. No one, surely, has splashed it down with such intelligence and panache as Bacon in these small, but uncompromising, paintings.

ANDREA ROSE
Director of Visual Arts, British Council

Bacon: Public and Private

RICHARD CALVOCORESSI

Now that Francis Bacon (1909–1992) has been dead for over a decade, and we can begin to form some sort of perspective on the twentieth century, the scale and significance of his achievement are becoming increasingly apparent. With the exception of Picasso and Andy Warhol, both of whom have museums dedicated to their life and work, we probably know more about Bacon than any other modern artist. This is ironic given how extensively Bacon edited his artistic past. But the gift, in 1998, of his London studio and its contents to the city of Dublin and its faithful reconstruction in the Hugh Lane Gallery, have transformed Bacon studies. Some 7,500 items were discovered in the studio, where the artist lived and worked for over thirty years, and the gallery has catalogued and entered every single one onto a special database. These entries give a unique insight into Bacon's eclectic sources, preoccupations and working methods.

A handful of exhibitions has been staged in the last three or four years exemplifying this new, analytical approach to Bacon's art, culminating in the magisterial *Francis Bacon and the Tradition of Art* (Vienna and Basel, 2003–4). This examined the full range of Bacon's work in the context of those artists from European high culture whom he appropriated and assimilated – Michelangelo, Velázquez, Rembrandt, Ingres, Degas, Van Gogh, Picasso – as well as the motifs and subjects that obsessed him: papal imagery; curtains and veils; the open mouth; the cage; circular forms, spaces and structures; the male human body; portraiture; mirrors and reflections; the shadow; the Crucifixion; meat and flesh. More recently, Martin Harrison in his book *In Camera* has revealed the extent to which Bacon based many of his most memorable images on 'low art' sources such as photographs and film-stills torn from books, magazines and newspapers. In his interviews with David Sylvester from the early 1960s onwards, Bacon readily admitted his debt to the great art of the past, which he knew only in reproduction, and often referred to his use of Eadweard Muybridge's sequential photographs of human figures and animals in action. But Harrison draws attention to a stratum of less elevated imagery which fascinated Bacon and which his friend the painter and photographer Peter Rose Pulham called 'bad Press photographs reproduced through a coarse screen on bad paper'.[1] Harrison also convincingly points to an obscure German book on spiritualism, with trick photographs of ectoplasms, emanations and other psychic phenomena, as an important source which the artist did not acknowledge; a paint spattered and well-thumbed copy was found in Bacon's studio.

Bacon liked the news photograph because it was instantaneous and to a large degree reliant on chance. In its fluidity and suppression of detail, it suggested transmutation and flux – qualities he tried to capture in his own radical manipulation of paint. David Sylvester, in a lecture on the artist (given in 2001 but not published until this year), argues that the main reason Bacon worked from the photographic image rather than from life was that 'it is easier to make a flat image … based on the observation of an existing flat image than it is to make a flat image … based on the observation of something in the round'.[2] In other words, Bacon, who lacked the traditional art-school training of painting or drawing from a living model, found that photographs had already done some of the work of translating three-dimensional form into two-dimensional form for him. Bacon painted a small number of portraits from life in the 1950s but from the early 1960s preferred to work from commissioned photographs of friends and lovers which functioned as a kind of aide-memoire while he tried to imagine their presence on canvas. Their actual presence in the studio, he claimed, would have inhibited his freedom to 'distort'.

Until recently, Sylvester's series of conversations with the artist, first published in 1975 and twice expanded in the 1980s, was one of the most quoted texts on any twentieth-century artist. *Interviews with Francis Bacon* ('surely the richest discussions between artist and critic ever re-corded', in the words of the painter and writer Andrew Forge)[3] helped make Bacon a public figure, or at least a very public kind of artist, in his lifetime. Shortly before his death in 2001, Sylvester published *Looking back at Francis Bacon*, a collection of essays, thoughts and new biographical material to which he added previously unpublished extracts from his recorded interviews with the artist. In one section, 'Bacon's secret vice', Sylvester was forced to correct the impression, which Bacon himself had been careful to promote in their conversations, that the artist never made preliminary studies before starting a painting; over seventy rapid, perfunctory sketches were found in Bacon's studio before it was transported to Dublin. Bacon also made lists of ideas for paintings on scraps of paper and on the inside covers of books. But both categories should be seen as substitutes for fully worked-out compositional studies in the same way that photo-graphs were – including photographic reproductions of his own work, which Bacon increasingly 'quoted' as he got older. So, in spite of such minor 'economies with the truth', *Interviews with Francis Bacon* will remain an essential resource for many years to come, especially when read in conjunction with Sylvester's final revisions and reflections on this most profound and complex of painters.

There is another, more obvious sense in which Bacon was a public artist. From 1962 until his death thirty years later, he released into the world, at the rate of almost one a year, twenty-eight large triptychs: that is to say, canvases each nearly two metres high by one and a half metres wide, grouped in threes – eighty-four panels in total. Each panel usually contains a centrally-placed figure, or a pair of coupled figures, alive with painterly incident, set off against broad, flat expanses of thinly applied colour that appear to parody abstract painting. Although presented serially, the narrative link between each panel is not always clear, if indeed it exists. A number of these triptychs hang in prominent museums around the world, where they are difficult to ignore: like the medieval or Renaissance altarpiece from which their format derives, they imply portentous, if highly ambiguous, public statements. Many of them address archetypal subjects, such as violent death, sexual ecstasy (and their interconnection), mutability and loss, and invoke earlier treatments of these themes in classical Greek tragedy, Christian iconography and the poetry of T.S. Eliot. A few incorporate images of contemporary political figures or events. Even when they have a commemorative purpose, as in those recalling Bacon's deceased lover George Dyer, there is something theatrical about them, reinforced by the spaces in which their dramas are enacted, like stages or arenas, which presuppose an audience. As Sylvester commented, 'Bacon had something of Picasso's genius for transforming his autobiography into images with a mythic allure and weight'.[4]

But there was another side to Bacon. The majority of images in this exhibition are of heads, slightly under life-size and seen from close to. They are painted on small canvases, each fourteen by twelve inches (35.5×30.5cm), a format which Bacon seems to have settled on in 1961. Beginning in 1962, with *Study for Three Heads* (28), in which Bacon's own head is flanked by images of his lover Peter Lacy, who had recently died, these small canvases are often grouped in threes. The triptych form allowed Bacon to show different aspects of the same face or to contrast images of three different people (including, sometimes, himself). Almost all of the small heads are of individuals whom the artist knew extremely well, such as lovers and close friends.

The qualities of improvisation and immediacy, which Bacon valued so highly, are evident in the smeared and broken brushstrokes of these small portraits, and in their passages of vivid, non-naturalistic colour, in a way that is not always apparent in the large triptychs, with their symmetrical structure and more formalised imagery. In Bacon's heads, image and paint are inextricably fused; as one of Bacon's strongest admirers, the painter Michael Andrews, observed, 'the object is *changed* into paint, not described in or with paint'.[5] These small paintings open up a rich vein of intimacy in Bacon's art; they are like private, devotional portraits, their blurred features evoking movement and irrepressible life but also, perhaps, dissolution and inevitable death. Portraying three contrasting views of the same subject may also indicate a conception of human identity as fluctuating and relative. This sense of a multiple self or selves is reinforced by the unfinished status of these portraits as implied by their titles: *Study for...*, *Study of...* and so on.

The exhibition also includes a number of larger, tonally painted heads and figures from the late 1940s and early 1950s, in which Bacon indulged his fascination with the open mouth, whether screaming or laughing hysterically; and portraits of blue-suited men from a monochrome series painted in 1954 which echoes the conventions of black and white studio photography. For a period in the late 1950s Bacon's output of portraits was dominated by the image of Peter Lacy, with whom he enjoyed a tense and often violent relationship but who, it has been claimed, was the 'love of his life'.[6] Lacy is the subject of five portraits in this exhibition, including two showing him asleep, which are remarkable for their tenderness and poignancy. Finally, the exhibition contains a handful of full-length portraits from the 1960s, their subjects shown standing, seated or reclining. Looking at these works one can understand what Andrews meant when he praised Bacon's 'realism of palpable presence'[7] – so real that you feel someone is in the room with you.

Sixty years ago, as Europe emerged from a debilitating world war which tested to the limit people's faith in humanist values, the Austrian painter Oskar Kokoschka (pioneer of the modern, psychological portrait) reflected pessimistically from his London exile on the future of portraiture.

Modern portrait painting has become a difficult task since the artist who tries to make people see the human being invisible in the present man is apt to make a fool of himself. Since humanism is dead, man is soul-less, he no longer cares if he lives or dies... There will be no portrait left of modern man because he has lost face and is turning back towards the jungle.[8]

As the extent of the physical and psychological damage caused by war and atrocity became known, many artists in Britain and on the Continent found it difficult to represent man as a secure, integrated being and turned instead – as Kokoschka predicted – to various less problematical alternatives such as abstraction.

A small group of painters and sculptors, however, ignored fashion and accepted the challenge of reinvigorating figurative art. For some, a renewed interest in anthropology and the art of 'primitive' societies gave them a precedent for the kind of expressive figuration they were looking for, uncontaminated by western 'civilization'.[9] Elsewhere, the new anthropocentrism tended to emphasise man's destructive potential or his resilience in the face of appalling suffering, his capacity for survival. Animal, bird and insect metaphors were sometimes used to suggest these forces; or else the human head and body would be depicted in extreme situations – disintegrating, wounded, terrified and so on. Bacon's crying or shouting heads of the late 1940s, with their sense of a person trapped by his or her animal instincts, can legitimately be read in this context. His later portraits of named or known individuals, however, have the effect of revealing 'the human being invisible in the present man' and restoring to him not only a face – or faces – but also a fragile sense of dignity. In this respect Bacon may be said to have reinvented portraiture for the post-humanist age.

1. Martin Harrison, *In Camera. Francis Bacon: Photography, Film and the Practice of Painting*, London, 2005, p.109.

2. David Sylvester, 'Francis Bacon and the Nude', in *Francis Bacon: Studying Form*, Faggionato Fine Art, London, 2005, p.18.

3. Andrew Forge, 'About Bacon', in *Francis Bacon*, Tate Gallery, London, 1985, p.24.

4. David Sylvester, *Looking Back at Francis Bacon*, London, 2000, p.186.

5. Michael Andrews, Unpublished notes on Francis Bacon written for Bruce Bernard, 1988 (Tate Archive).

6. John Edwards, quoted in Martin Harrison, *In Camera*, p.223.

7. Andrews, Unpublished notes.

8. Oskar Kokoschka, 'The Portrait in the Past and Present', in *Oskar Kokoschka: Vorträge, Aufsätze, Essays zur Kunst*, Hamburg, 1975, pp.147–9.

9. '... at present nobody can be feeling particularly proud of being civilised. Indeed, it is even possible to be somewhat envious of the world's simpler peoples, more concerned as they are to make friends with Nature than to seek to overcome their fellow-man. Nor has the artist himself any special reason to rejoice in civilisation in its most recent phase ...': from foreword (by R.R. Marett) to L. Adam, *Primitive Art*, Harmondsworth, 1940, p.7.

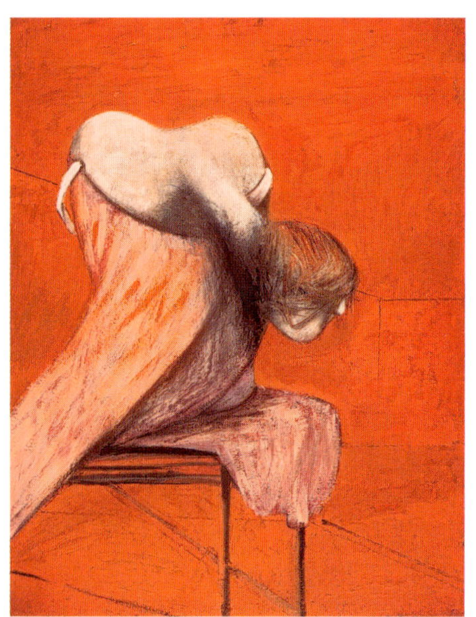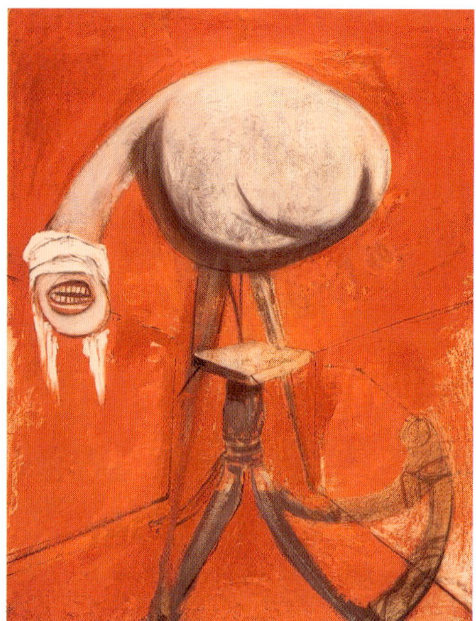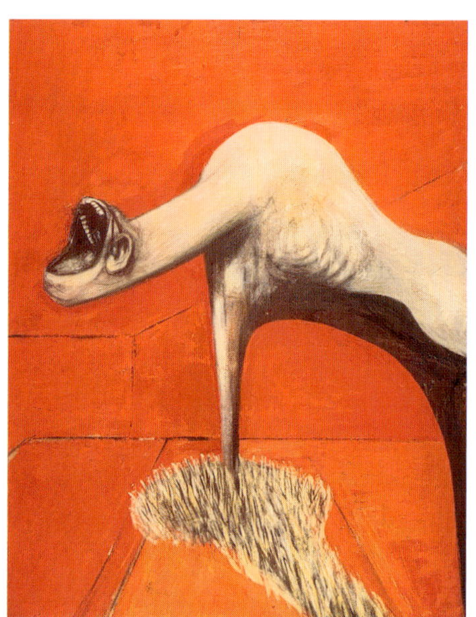

Fig. 1 | Francis Bacon, *Three Studies for Figures at the Base of a Crucifixion*, 1944
Tate, London

Clearing Away the Screens

MARTIN HAMMER

People tend to have quite a stereotyped view of Francis Bacon. The distortions of the human figure in his art are commonly taken as degrading, even repellent. It is said that Bacon's pictures express, in the guise of a universal truth about 'the human condition', a dark mentality specific to his generation, which experienced the Blitz, the pictures and newsreels of the Nazi death camps, the first use of the atom bomb in Japan, and the menace of the Cold War. John Berger, formerly a harsh critic, has recently described Bacon as the 'prophet of a pitiless world', a world after 9/11 characterised by 'ubiquitous indifference' and 'a conformism of fear': 'He repeatedly painted the human body or parts of the body in discomfort or agony or want. Sometimes the pain involved looks as if it has been inflicted; more often it seems to originate from within, from the guts of the body itself, from the misfortune of being physical.'[1] Bacon's bleak 'message' coexists incongruously with his old-fashioned commitment to oil paint, in canvases of old masterly scale, glazed and expensively framed. The recurrent triptych format comes across as Bacon's vehicle for projecting surrogate, even blasphemous, altarpieces, suited to a nihilistic society devoid of spirituality and any lingering sense of human dignity.

Such readings go back to the time of Bacon's initial emergence. The artist established his fundamental identity as a painter in his 1944 *Three Studies for Figures at the Base of a Crucifixion* (fig.1), bizarre hybrids of human and animal imagery that embody wartime sensations of fear, pain and despair. When this and another work were included in a commercial exhibition in April 1945, the critical reaction set the tone for things to come. The end of the Second World War was finally in view, but these pictures seemed to express Bacon's 'sense of the atrocious world into which we have survived', which made them 'symbols of outrage rather than works of art'.[2] His acclaimed solo exhibition at the Hanover Gallery, London in late 1949 struck one critic as 'the most profoundly disquieting manifestation I have yet seen of that malaise which, since the last war, has inspired the philosophy of Sartre and the drama of frustration of Tennessee Williams'.[3] Such comparisons may prompt us to understand Bacon's work in relation not only to idiosyncratic, personal impulses, but also to attitudes that were more widely current.

The clichés about his art capturing the spirit of the age do not tell the whole story. The same is true of the popular, not to say mythic, version of Bacon's biography. Here, reinforcing the impression of a warped, brutal sensibility behind the work, we encounter a quintessential outsider, a hard-drinking Soho bohemian immersed in a murky world of masochistic homosexual practices and affairs with dubious low-life characters. Yet the man who emerges from Michael Peppiatt's detailed chronicle is more complex.[4]

After a few drinks, we gather, Bacon could indeed be waspish; his friends 'could never be sure of coming though an evening with their sense of themselves unscathed'. In his later years, especially, he was capable of outrageous barbs against fellow artists, and it is no surprise that he fell out with old friends such as Graham Sutherland and Lucian Freud. And yet, one learns, Bacon devoted large sums to ensuring that close friends, such as the photographer John Deakin and the writers Sonia Orwell and Ann Fleming, approached their imminent deaths in luxurious surroundings, with the best possible medical care and/or champagne available to ease their passage. In such circumstances, Bacon could be kindness itself. Peppiatt further recalls how he might 'rush off to tend an old friend of his dead nanny's or make a large, anonymous contribution to a cause he thought worthwhile'. Bacon 'would spend hours subtly coaxing a friend out of a depression', extending a hospitality 'so lavish that it almost became comical'. Deakin commented revealingly about a photograph of the painter made around 1950: 'I like my picture of Francis Bacon enormously, perhaps because I like him so much, and admire his strange, tormented painting. He's an odd one, wonderfully tender and generous by nature, yet with curious streaks of cruelty, especially to his friends.'[5]

The present exhibition suggests that we need to take a similarly nuanced view of Bacon's art. It concentrates on his images of the human head and portraits, types that blur into one another in that the anonymous heads or figures were often conceived by the artist as, in some sense, portraits of specific individuals, and it seems arbitrary whether titles acknowledge this. Many of the works are also small in scale, which even extends to triptychs and other groupings. Together, portraiture and modest size suggest intimacy, as a description both of the relationship between artist and person portrayed, and of the encounter between viewer and work of art. Yet how can intimacy and the apparent brutality of Bacon's distortions be understood in tandem with one another, as Deakin declared the man to be at once tender and cruel?

Head and portrait formats were a constant preoccupation in Bacon's work. It is impossible to know how much he experimented with such imagery in the 1930s, as so little survived the artist's culling of his early production. However, the pastel from *c*.1931–2 (1) suggests a precocious interest, and its delicate modelling, dark backdrop, and poignant, even sentimental mood transport us directly to the late *Self-Portrait* of 1987 (39), as if his art had come full circle. An interest in the portrait certainly persisted throughout Bacon's post-war career. We know that he was drawn to the genre from his letters, written in 1946, to Graham Sutherland from the south of France. Bacon was, we discover, working already on variants of the great Velázquez portrait of *Pope Innocent X* (fig.2), which subsequently led to the 1949 *Head VI* (4) and many more Pope pictures thereafter. This enthusiasm seems to have prompted experimentation of his own:

> *I don't know how the copy of the Velázquez will turn out. I have practically finished one I think and am going to start on a portrait I want to do, but it is thrilling to paint from a picture which really excites you. I am sick to death of everything I've ever done in the past but continue to think like a child or a fool that I'm on the edge of doing a good painting.*[6]

Another letter, relaying his experiences in Paris, suggests the spirit in which he embarked upon portraiture. A big international survey of contemporary art was dismissed for 'the boring lack of reality, the lack of immediacy which we have so often talked about… It is the terrible decoration we are all contaminated by.' As an antidote, Bacon was looking forward to a Balthus exhibition, but this too proved disappointing:

> *They are no good. He is trying to get the tenderness which we would all love to get for a change, but it can't be done that way, it can only come as a technical thing and not as illustration or at least I feel that. I feel more and more that nothing matters or will happen until someone makes a new technical synthesis that can carry over from the sensation to our nervous system.*[7]

The impulse towards technical experiment, in the pursuit of conveying feeling without the mediation of the intellect, continued to be a pressing concern. One might further argue that Bacon's portraiture stemmed from just such an ambition to encapsulate 'the tenderness which we would all love to get for a change'.

Nothing survives between a group of works from early 1946 and the *Head* series and related pictures which dominated Bacon's Hanover Gallery exhibition three years later. Although the title *Head* suggests something more generalised, these pictures were subsequently described by the critic John Russell as a knowing inversion of what we usually understand by portraiture:

> *Looking at them, we realise that although European painting includes a great many portraits of individuals in rooms, they are never about what it feels like to be alone in a room: the painter always makes two … The garbage of the psyche has been put out at the back door; all buttons are done up … What painting had never shown before is the disintegration of the social being which takes place when one is alone in a room which has no looking glass. We may feel at such times that the accepted hierarchy of our features is collapsing, and that we are by turns all teeth, all eye, all ear, all nose.*[8]

Russell's existentialist reading complements the parallels to Bacon's pictorial imagery evident in *Nausea* by Jean-Paul Sartre. The novel appeared in 1938 and in English translation in early 1949.[9] In a passage early on, the narrator undergoes an experience of 'nausea', meaning the alarming sensation of things breaking loose from their comforting names and categories, and assuming a viscous

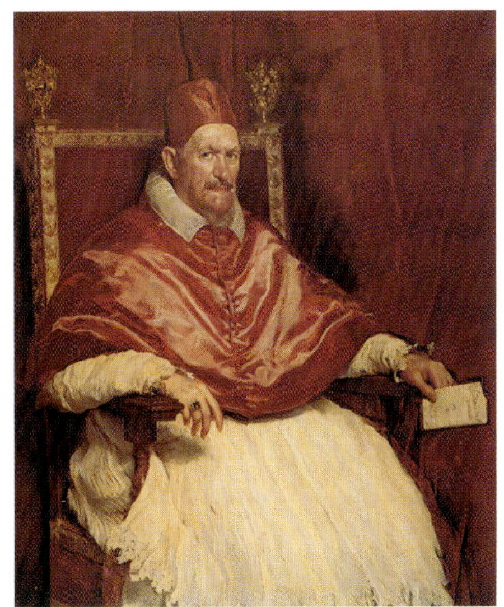

Fig.2 | Diego Velázquez, *Pope Innocent X*, 1650
Galleria Doria-Pamphili, Rome

presence as matter. In Sartre's philosophical formulation, existence precedes essence – things and indeed persons are stuff and raw possibility, before we choose to fix and so diminish them. Thus the central character, Antoine Roquentin, is sitting at his desk, alone, when he catches sight of his own features:

> *It is a trap. I know I am going to let myself be caught in it. I have. The grey thing appears in the mirror. I go over and look at it, I can no longer get away ... My glance slowly and wearily travels over my forehead, my cheeks. It finds nothing firm ... When I was little, my Aunt Bigeois told me 'If you look at yourself too long in the mirror, you'll see a monkey.' I must have looked at myself even longer than that: what I see is well below the monkey, on the fringe of the vegetable world, at the level of jellyfish ... The eyes especially are horrible seen so close. They are glassy, soft, blind, red-rimmed, they look like fish scales ... I would like to take hold of myself: an acute, vivid sensation would deliver me. I plaster my left hand against my cheek, I pull the skin; I grimace at myself. An entire half of my face yields, the left half of the mouth twists and swells, uncovering a tooth, the eye opens on a white globe, on pink, bleeding flesh. That is not what I was looking for: nothing strong, nothing new; soft, flaccid, stale!*[10]

We seem to have here not just a contemporary equivalent to the 1949 pictures, but also a literary anticipation of Bacon's treatment of the human features in general, where flesh often seems to be dissolving, a sensation heightened by the deliberate contrast with the hard forms of teeth and glasses, as well as the space frames and stark geometric interiors that frequently serve to contain, even imprison, his figures. Taking our cue from Sartre, it may be that we should read the distortions in Bacon less as tokens of violence visited upon his sitters by the artist than as emanations of the sitters' own private, elemental sense of being, at moments when the social façade is stripped away.

A further parallel between artist and writer was their fascination with the tradition of obsequious, official portraiture. Elsewhere in *Nausea* Roquentin describes his experiences when visiting a local museum. The serried ranks of local worthies, meticulously described in all their finery and with all their attributes of status, induce a growing sense of alienation. In the eyes of a merchant, he reads a 'calm, implacable judgement' which '... pierced me like a sword and called in question my very right to exist ... I had appeared by chance, I existed like a stone, a plant, a microbe. My life grew in a haphazard way and in all directions ...'[11] Subsequently, he begins to see through the idealising conventions, especially as he becomes fixated upon a picture of Jean Parrotin:

> *I knew, as a result of contemplating for a long time a certain portrait of Philip II in the library of the Escurial, that, when you look straight at a face ablaze with a sense of privilege, this fire dies out after a moment, and only an ashy residue remains: it was this residue which interested me.*
>
> *Parrotin put up a good fight. But all of a sudden, the light in his eyes went out, the picture grew dim.*
>
> *What was left? Blind eyes, a mouth as thin as a dead snake, and cheeks. The pale round cheeks of a child: they spread out over the canvas... How long had it taken his wife to notice them?... One day, I imagine, as her husband was sleeping beside her... she had ventured to look him in the face: all this flesh had appeared to her without any defence, bloated, slavering, vaguely obscene...*[12]

Likewise, in the work of Bacon formulaic portraiture comprised the other side of the coin. *Head VI* of 1949 (4) flagrantly dismantles a pictorial embodiment of power and privilege. It is as though the Pope Innocent X we know, and are duly overawed by, has dissolved before our eyes – the picture has grown dim, and the light in his eyes has assuredly gone out, veiled by streaks of dry black paint, dragged and scumbled across the coarse canvas, which constitute an exact visual parallel to Sartre's 'ashy residue'. From close to, the paint looks very like a deposit of soot.

The 1949 *Study for Portrait* (7) bears a particular affinity to *Head VI*. Over and above the open-mouthed heads, and the inclusion around both figures of a spatial cage, the two works are very close technically. But the Chicago picture is the first surviving work that Bacon explicitly presented as a portrait, although without the title viewers might be hard pressed so to identify the picture. One can only speculate whether, for Bacon himself, *Study for Portrait* captured the essence of an unidentified individual. The picture may anticipate his portrayal of Lucian Freud in 1951 by appropriating a photograph of the writer Franz Kafka; famously, Freud came to Bacon's studio to be painted, only to find that the picture was already finished (8). Perhaps *Study for Portrait* also started off as a transcription of a ready-made image, such as a snapshot, film still, news photograph of a trial, or even an execution by electric chair. Whether or not there was a specific source, *Study for Portrait* registers the moment at which Bacon's art becomes more overtly photographic, both in the relative naturalism of his figure style and in the unmistakable reference to the blur and graininess of the imagery that we know he found so stimulating in magazines like *Time* and *Picture Post*.

A more direct approach to recording the look and aura of particular individuals emerges in Bacon's work around 1953–4, in pictures that are variously described as studies for portraits, figures or simply as *Man in Blue* (11–14). The latter were apparently based on a man Bacon encountered at a hotel. Otherwise, Bacon remarked that the dark, blurred pictures of suited male figures set in claustrophobic interiors were generally 'done of somebody who was always in a state of unease ... very neurotic and almost hysterical'.[13] This presumably referred to Peter Lacy, with whom Bacon was involved in an intense and often traumatic affair in the mid-1950s. Lacy was probably the subject of the highly abbreviated *Head in Grey* of 1955 (24). The more muted colour and atmosphere of this body of work mark a new departure, culminating in the extreme simplicity and pathos of the 1955 *Study for Portrait II (after the Life Mask of William Blake)* (15). Judging from the title, memories or observations of some particular individual fused in Bacon's imagination with looking at photographs of the cast features of the artist. He was perhaps drawn to the ambiguity of the mask – it was, in a sense, both a life and a death mask. That ambiguity is articulated visually in Bacon's picture through the extraordinary smearing technique he improvised, suggesting the form of the head but also its potential dissolution.[14]

The portraits of the mid-1950s, with their frontally positioned sitters, framing devices, dark tonalities and streaked paint application, recall the images of his wife and brother that Alberto Giacometti had been producing in Paris since the late 1940s (figs.3 & 4). The comparison extends not only to the paintings and drawings but also to Giacometti's roughly textured sculptures, where the emphatic delineation of contours and features is echoed in Bacon's notably sculptural, but at the same time fugitive *Study for Portrait II (after the Life Mask of William Blake)*. A major Giacometti exhibition was in fact mounted in London in the summer of 1955. The catalogue strikingly reveals how many works in all media had been accumulated in Britain over recent years, by the Tate Gallery, for example, as well as by private collectors who were also in

many cases Bacon supporters, such as Peter Watson, proprietor of *Horizon* magazine where the first critical essay on Bacon had appeared; Robert Sainsbury, who commissioned Bacon to paint himself and his wife that same year; and John Hewett, a dealer who met Bacon in 1955 and sold many works by both artists.[15] Above all, the show had been organised by David Sylvester, a close friend of Bacon's and by now his most prominent critical advocate. For Sylvester, Bacon and Giacometti were the twin exemplars of the possibility of a new, existential mode of figurative realism. Sylvester might equally have been talking about Bacon in certain passages in his essay in the catalogue that accompanied the Giacometti exhibition: 'Shadow and substance, life and death – images flickering in and out of the mind … Life passes, and awareness of nostalgia. This is what Giacometti's sculptures may – among other things – be thought to be saying, and therein

20

Fig. 3 | Alberto Giacometti, *Diego Seated*, 1949
Tate, London

Fig. 4 | Alberto Giacometti, *Large Head of Diego*, 1954
Alberto Giacometti Foundation, Zurich

Fig. 5 | Edgar Degas, *Diego Martelli*, 1879
National Gallery of Scotland, Edinburgh

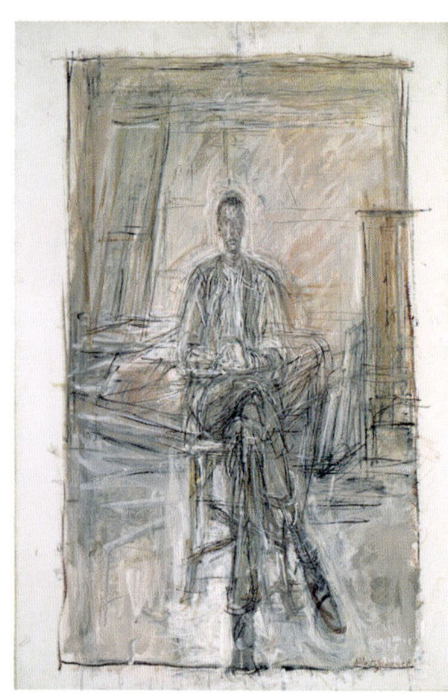

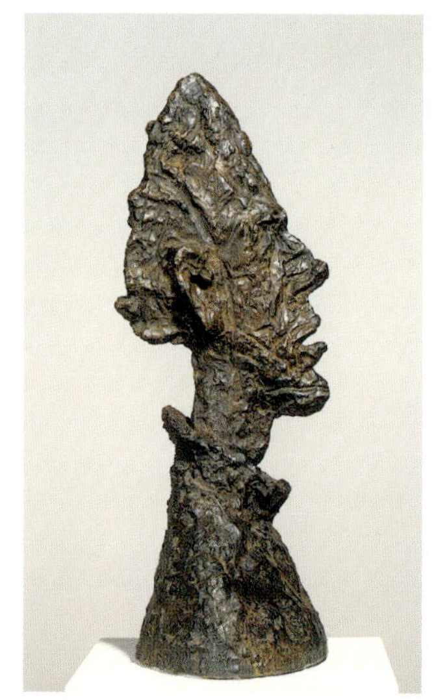

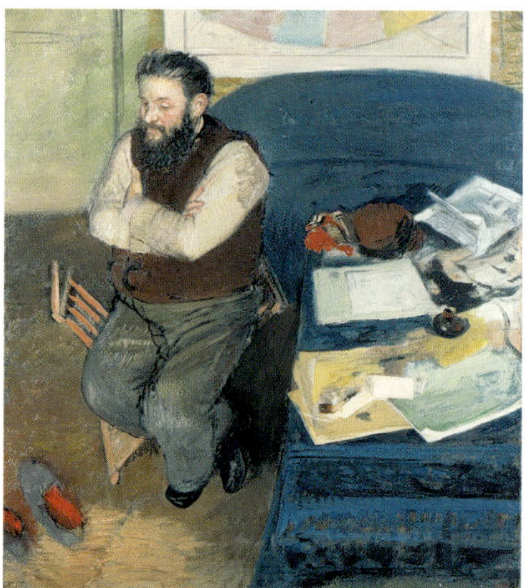

lies their poignancy … Their sense of the transitory is a sense of loss.'[16]

Towards the end of the decade, after the explosion of colour in his Van Gogh variations, Bacon arrived at the idiom that underpinned his entire subsequent work. In essence, whole or partial figures, described in terms of strong contours containing passages of increasingly fluid, painterly brushwork, are played off against flat, thinly painted props and backdrops, whether dark or bright in tone or colour, causing the main subjects to project more emphatically than before. The transition is exemplified by works such as the 1958 *Lying Figure* (25) and, from the following year, *Sleeping Figure* (26) and *Miss Muriel Belcher* (18). The 1963 Cardiff self-portrait (33) is typical of Bacon's mature style. It also possesses interesting affinities with Degas's *Diego Martelli* in the National Gallery of Scotland (fig.5).[17] Cumulatively, the casual pose, three-quarter view of the head, props like the discarded newspaper and ashtray, the simple, curvilinear blue sofa, even the prominent footwear viewed face on, suggest that Bacon may have been looking at this particular work. An interest in Degas would be symptomatic of Bacon's increasing sense of himself as a realist artist, committed to the representation of actualities rather than 'expressionist' excesses. His decision to stop making Pope paintings was accompanied by vehement assertions that he now disliked the entire series: 'When I was young I needed extreme subject-matter for my paintings. Then as I grew older I began to find my subject-matter in my own life.'[18]

Bacon now embarked upon his most sustained exploration of the portrait genre. Several were presented anonymously, but from the early 1960s onwards, many pictures were explicitly devoted to a cluster of named individuals. His recurrent sitters were intimate personal friends or lovers and included the artists Lucian Freud and Isabel Rawsthorne, Muriel Belcher from the Colony Room in Soho, Henrietta Moraes, another drinking companion, the French writer and critic Michel Leiris, wildlife photographer Peter Beard, and East Enders George Dyer and John Edwards. Perhaps his greatly increased commercial and critical success in this period, especially after the big Tate Gallery retrospective of 1962, meant that Bacon no longer felt inhibited about being seen to engage with a genre ostensibly more bound up with tradition than modern art. Self-portraiture became an especially strong theme in the 1970s. Bacon provided a straightforward explanation: 'people around me have been dying like flies and I've had nobody else left to paint but myself'.[19] There was, however, a downside to this ready availability: 'I loathe my own face' was another regular utterance.

The portraiture from these decades falls into several types, although the size of the heads varies little between the numerous small pictures, occasional half-lengths, and full-length pictures where the inclusion of settings generates a more theatrical atmosphere. All of the people mentioned, as well as anonymous sitters like the man with glasses and Bacon himself, feature in an extended series of pictures measuring 35.5 × 30.5cm (14 × 12 inches). They focus straightforwardly on the head and shoulders, and impose a relatively consistent simplification of the features in terms of rhymed curvilinear shapes. Given the similarities, it is remarkable how the different individuals seem to exude their own singular presence. Between the 1976 and 1987 portraits of Michel Leiris and John Edwards, for example, there are considerable similarities of technique and artistic language. There is also a gulf not only of the eleven years that elapsed between Bacon's execution of the two pictures, but also in the aura given off by the images of the two men, an aged Parisian intellectual and a youthful working-class East Ender. The inwardness of the one and the physicality of the other are vividly conveyed. According to Russell, 'anyone who knows even one of the sitters' will agree that 'individual aspects of the sitter are shown to us … with an intensity not often encountered in life'; the pictures stand up as 'representations of known persons'.[20]

Such paintings also depart radically from conventional or photographic representation, and reflect Bacon's immersion in artistic possibilities opened up by the work of Picasso. In the Leiris portrait, for example, Bacon seems to have reinvented in his own terms the effects of semi-transparency, and the interplay between likeness and autonomy of pictorial structure, that characterise the Cubist portraits by Picasso of 1910. Sylvester detected in the 1963 *Portrait of Man with Glasses III* (22) an echo of Picasso's images of Jaime Sabartés from 1939.[21] Yet one senses that Bacon's portraits, more than Picasso's, embody concerns to capture appearances, through the observation of distinctive features and body language, and to convey character or presence, that are familiar from the history of portraiture. In particular, they rehearse a tradition of psychologically probing portraiture that is epitomised by Rembrandt, who ranked not far behind Velázquez in Bacon's personal pantheon (fig.6).[22]

Fig.6 | Rembrandt van Rijn, *Self-portrait aged Fifty-one,* 1657
National Gallery of Scotland, Edinburgh on loan from the Duke of Sutherland

Fig.7 | Sir Anthony van Dyck, *Charles I in Three Positions*
The Royal Collection © 2005, Her Majesty Queen Elizabeth II

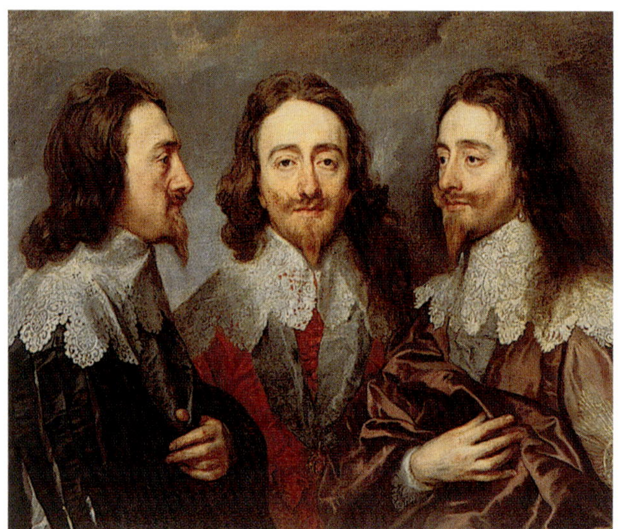

On occasion, the head and shoulder pictures were grouped into triptychs portraying a single person, or occasionally two or three different sitters, running in parallel to the series of big triptychs that emerged during this period. When we are presented with three images of Freud, Rawsthorne, Moraes, or Bacon, we are invited to compare and contrast, and to accumulate a sense of the variety of inner and outer aspects of a complex individual. We may make subliminal associations with Van Dyck's three combined images of King Charles I (fig.7), made for the benefit of a remote sculptor, or indeed with a small, private altarpiece – either reinforces the attitude of affection for his sitters that Bacon seems to project. At the same time, we know that police mug shots and photo booth pictures were types of vernacular imagery that fascinated Bacon. In his own pictures, the heroic and the banal are held in exquisite tension.

The 1966 *Portrait of Isabel Rawsthorne* (49) epitomises Bacon's technical methods. Close inspection suggests myriad ways of applying paint in the transcription of the figure, set off by a flat, matt backdrop that was probably applied last, concealing the evidence of adjustments and improvisation. Lines and areas of tone appear to be produced by brushwork, evoking the edges of forms and the play of cast shadows. But in the face, paint is dragged, almost caressed, across the weave of the canvas, and textured by what look like rubbing and dabbing with a cloth, and, in the case of the white blob to the right of the mouth, perhaps squeezing paint direct from the tube. Such distinctive and experimental techniques are elaborated throughout Bacon's portraiture of the period. The effect in the Rawsthorne picture is complex and considered, for all

the artist's assertions of his essential spontaneity. What comes across to the viewer is a suggestive ambiguity. The sitter appears still and solid, reminiscent of a classical bust, projecting a sideways gaze that is both imperious and watchful. Yet the accumulation of rhythmic, semi-transparent forms serves to dematerialise the figure, and to suggest a process of movement enacted by either sitter or observer. The picture moves in and out of naturalistic suggestion, but the most flagrant intervention is the blob of white, which we might wish to read as saliva, semen, or, less literally, as the token of some more generic human vitality emanating from artist, sitter, or both.

It is evident from such a picture that Bacon worked from memory, rather than with the sitter present, though he remarked that 'sometimes one needs to see the person, also, while one's painting'.[23] He also used photographs as his immediate point of reference. Bacon started around 1962 to employ photographs commissioned from John Deakin, whose work he greatly admired. In 1966, he stated:

> *… if I both know them and have photographs of them, I find it easier to work than actually having their presence in the room. I think that, if I have the presence of the image there, I am not able to drift so freely as I am able to through the photographic image. This may be just my own neurotic sense but I find it less inhibiting to work from them through memory and their photographs than actually having them seated there before me.*[24]

The term 'drifting' covers a rich array of possible interpretations that might be placed upon sitter or source image. In the case of *Portrait of Isabel Rawsthorne Standing in a Street in Soho* of 1967 (51), one can see how Deakin's informal, anecdotal imagery turns into something grand

and hieratic in Bacon's picture, so that the sitter assumes 'an almost tragic dignity'.[25] Excluding the normal transaction between artist and sitter is entirely compatible with a concern to express 'what it feels like to be alone in a room'. Moreover the photograph elides the distinction between the living and the dead. In the 1962 *Study for Three Heads* (28), a self-portrait in the centre is flanked by two images of Peter Lacy, news of whose death in Tangier Bacon had recently received.[26] A decade later, posthumous portraits of George Dyer, based once again on Deakin prototypes, served a similarly cathartic and commemorative purpose.

In the 1960s and 1970s Bacon submitted to the interrogations of David Sylvester, resulting in the remarkable volume of interviews. From scattered reflections and asides one can reconstruct the broad outlines of a philosophy of portraiture. Bacon's commitment to the genre is clear:

> BACON: *I think art is an obsession with life and after all, as we are human beings, our greatest obsession is with ourselves. Then possibly with animals, and then with landscapes.*
>
> SYLVESTER: *You're really affirming the traditional hierarchy of subject-matter by which history painting … comes top and then portraits and then landscape and then still life.*
>
> BACON: *I would alter them round. I would say at the moment, as things are so difficult, that portraits come first.*[27]

Why were things 'so difficult'? Most obviously, photography had taken over the descriptive functions of the genre. Furthermore, Bacon's ambitions for portraiture are remote from conventional kinds of characterisation, geared towards flattery and projecting the sitter's social façade through an assimilation of individual to type. Instead, he holds out for the possibility of a deeper penetration of an individual's singular mode of being. He commented: 'I couldn't do people I didn't know very well. I wouldn't want to. It wouldn't interest me to try to do them unless I had seen a lot of them, watched their contours, watched the way they behaved.'[28] In painting an individual, you are 'trying to get near not only to their appearance but also to the way they have affected you, because every shape has an implication'.[29] His aims in painting his intimate friends are conveyed in a later interview:

> *The living quality is what you have to get. In painting a portrait the problem is to find a technique by which you can give over all the pulsations of a person … Most people go to the most academic portrait painters when they want to have their portraits made because for some reason they prefer a kind of coloured photograph of themselves instead of having themselves really trapped and caught. The sitter is someone of flesh and blood and what has to be caught is their emanation.*[30]

Bacon stated that his fundamental concern was 'to distort the thing far beyond the appearance, but in the distortion to bring it back to a recording of the appearance'. The method by which this was done was highly 'artificial', and 'if I like them, I don't want to practice before them the injury I do to them in my work'. The sitter might have witnessed an exploratory process of building up marks, textures and shapes on the canvas, making more or less overt reference to representational detail, and with the artist moving back and forth, making adjustments and accepting or rejecting the configurations in front of him. Bacon exploited chance, cultivating ways of applying paint that evaded conscious control: 'one knows that by some accidental brushmarks suddenly appearance comes in with a vividness that no accepted way of doing it would have brought about'.[31] Indeed, he found that 'portraits are even more accidental than other types of painting I do', and stated that 'my ideal would be just to pick up a handful of paint and throw it at the canvas and hope that the portrait was there'.[32] The 1967 *Study for Head of Lucian Freud* (47) looks about as close as Bacon ever came to realising this goal. From the point of view of the spectator, he wanted to create 'portraits of people, but, when you come to analyze them, you just won't know – or it would be very hard to see – how the image is made up at all.' Illustration is equated with too obvious or banal a correspondence between the subject matter and the means of representation. Bacon's pursuit of improvisation, as the antidote, was 'very wearing':

> *… the other day I painted a head of somebody and what made the sockets of the eyes, the nose, the mouth were, when you analyzed them, just forms which had nothing to do with eyes, nose or mouth; but the paint moving from one contour into another made a likeness of this person I was trying to paint … the next day I tried to take it further and tried to make it more poignant, more near, and I lost the image completely. Because this kind of image is a kind of tightrope walk between what is called figurative painting and abstraction… It's an attempt to bring the figurative thing up onto the nervous system more violently and more poignantly.*[33]

This takes us to the heart of the ambition that Bacon held for his art in general: 'Isn't it that one wants a thing to be as factual as possible and at the same time as deeply suggestive or deeply unlocking of areas of sensation other than simply illustration of the object you set out to do?'[34]

Bacon presumably decided that a picture worked in his terms when it seemed to fuse vivid suggestions of the singular features and aura of an individual portrayed with qualities of formal order and rhythm, as well as more generalised intimations of movement and vitality, that had all emerged and crystallised within the creative process. Distortion, in the sense of deformation or caricature of the features of an individual, was a by-product rather than an intended effect:

> *Whether the distortions which I think sometimes bring the image over more violently are damage is a very questionable idea. I don't think it is damage. You may say it is damaging if you take it on the level of illustration. But not if you take it on the level of what I think of as art. One brings the sensation and the feeling of life over the only way he can.*[35]

The 'particular way of painting' to which Bacon aspired was:

> *more poignant than illustration… because it has a life of its own. It lives on its own, like the image one's trying to trap; it lives on its own, and therefore transfers the essence of the image more poignantly. So that the artist may be able to open up or rather, should I say, unlock the valves of feeling and therefore return the onlooker to life more violently.*[36]

When the coagulation of matter that constitutes a person is transmuted into a coagulation of paint on canvas, vitality may be captured, but the implied expenditure of energy evokes transience and the shadow of life, which is death. Thus, catching and, for the viewer, recognising a sense of life becomes poignant and emotionally violent.

Berger states that Bacon's figures communicate something of 'the misfortune of being physical', but he is surely wrong to state that the artist's standpoint is 'pitiless', as though the intention is to degrade or diminish his sitters. Rather, one might adapt the words of Deakin, to the effect that Bacon's portraits of his friends turn out, like his everyday behaviour towards them, to be 'wonderfully tender and generous' but 'with curious streaks of cruelty'. Loving and a sort of loathing – Bacon's professed attitude towards his own features – turn out to be two sides of the same coin. In his use of language, as in the pictures themselves, one constantly encounters ambiguity in Bacon's approach to portraiture. There is an aspiration to distil the specific pulsations that a given person gives off, implying an attitude of tenderness and empathy. At the same time, he wants portraits to trap his sitters, in the manner of a wildlife photographer, which sounds a more disengaged and threatening standpoint. His frequent recourse to photographs implies both an engagement with the specific appearance of the person, and also a detachment necessary to the underlying expressive purpose of his portraiture. The portraits embody Bacon's conviction that to express love or feeling for a person, even oneself, is not to project onto the features a spurious veneer of idealisation, but rather, if it could somehow be done, to include in one's representation suggestions of elemental vitality, carnality, subjection to instinct, mortality, human mutability and complexity, and the degree to which outer features conceal rather than disclose inner life. All this and more might be accommodated within the notion of 'the pulsations of a person'.

To communicate such feelings and perceptions sounds difficult indeed. Yet the artist believed that something of Peter Lacy's fraught temperament may have 'come across' in the 1950s portraits: 'I've always hoped to put over things as directly and rawly as I possibly can … if you say something very directly to somebody, they're sometimes offended, although it is a fact. Because people tend to be offended by facts, or what used to be called truth.'[37] In one final passage from his conversations with Sylvester, Bacon again denied that his preoccupation as an artist, and as a portrait painter especially, was to shock or wilfully distort. Uncomfortable realities might be at stake, but his portraiture would only seem inhumane to those cocooned in fantasy:

When I look at you across the table, I don't only see you but I see a whole emanation, which has to do with personality and everything else. And to put that over in a painting, as I would like to be able to do in a portrait, means that it would appear violent in paint. We nearly always live through screens – a screened existence. And I sometimes think, when people say my work looks violent, that perhaps I have from time to time been able to clear away one or two of the veils or screens.[38]

1. John Berger, 'Prophet of a pitiless world', *The Guardian*, review section, 29 May 2004.

2. Cited in Michael Peppiatt, *Francis Bacon: Anatomy of an Enigma*, London, 1996, p.109.

3. Neville Wallis, 'Nightmare', *The Observer*, 20 November 1949.

4. Peppiatt, *Francis Bacon*. The following paragraph draws on material from pp.243–4, 283–4 and 291–3.

5. *Ibid.*, p.160.

6. The originals are in the Sutherland archive held by the National Museums and Galleries of Wales, Cardiff, and the entire correspondence is transcribed in Martin Hammer, *Bacon and Sutherland,* New Haven and London, 2005.

7. See note 6.

8. John Russell, *Francis Bacon*, London, 1979, p.38.

9. Jean-Paul Sartre, *The Diary of Antoine Roquentin*, London, 1949, translated by Lloyd Alexander (hereafter *Nausea*).

10. *Ibid.*, pp.27–8.

11. *Ibid.*, p.124.

12. *Ibid.*, pp.130–1.

13. David Sylvester, *Interviews with Francis Bacon*, London, 1993, p.48.

14. On the background to this group of works, see Martin Harrison, *In Camera. Francis Bacon: Photography, Film and the Practice of Painting,* London, 2005, pp.133–4.

15. See catalogue for *Alberto Giacometti*, Arts Council Gallery, St James's Square, 4 June – 9 July 1955. The Tate is given as the owner of three works, Peter Watson of three, Robert Sainsbury of eleven, and K.J. Hewett of nine. Mrs E. Molesworth was the most richly endowed of several further British private collectors. On Bacon's connection with Hewett see David Sylvester, *Looking Back at Francis Bacon*, London, 2000, p.112.

16. David Sylvester, 'Perpetuating the Transient', *Alberto Giacometti*, n.p.. Sylvester is also listed as the owner of two drawings. His later essay 'Bacon and Giacometti' is included in *Looking Back*, pp.194–204. On Giacometti's general influence at this time in Britain, see James Hyman, *The Battle for Realism*, New Haven and London, 2001, pp.152–3, and, with more specific reference to the late 1940s work of Bacon, Hammer, *Bacon and Sutherland,* chp.3.

17. It is perhaps relevant that J.S. Boggs's book *Degas and Portraiture* appeared in 1962. Bacon was a great devourer of illustrated art books. Degas was a general source of inspiration. The radical approach to the image of the naked human body in Degas's pictures of girls at their toilette was clearly one starting point for the 1964 triptych, *Three Figures in a Room*, Musée National d'Art Moderne, Centre Georges Pompidou, Paris.

18. Cited in Peppiatt, *Francis Bacon*, p.207.

19. Sylvester, *Interviews,* p.129.

20. Russell, *Francis Bacon*, p.124.

21. Sylvester, *Looking Back*, pp.92–3.

22. See Alexandra Hennig, 'Francis Bacon: Portraiture after Representation', W. Seipel, B. Steffen, C. Vitali (eds.), *Francis Bacon and the Tradition of Art*, Milan, 2004, pp.215–20.

23. Sylvester, *Interviews,* p.144.

24. *Ibid.*, p.40.

25. The phrase comes from Colm Tóibín's thought-provoking essay on Bacon (*Love in a Dark Time. Gay Lives from Wilde to Almodóvar,* London, 2001, p.159).

26. Sylvester, *Looking Back*, p.111.

27. Sylvester, *Interviews,* p.63.

28. *Ibid.*, pp.73–4.

29. *Ibid.*, p.130.

30. *Ibid.*, p.174.

31. *Ibid.*, p.105.

32. *Ibid.*, pp.136 and 107.

33. *Ibid.*, pp.11–12.

34. *Ibid.*, p.56.

35. *Ibid.*, pp.42–3.

36. *Ibid.*, p.17.

37. *Ibid.*, p.48.

38. *Ibid.*, p.82.

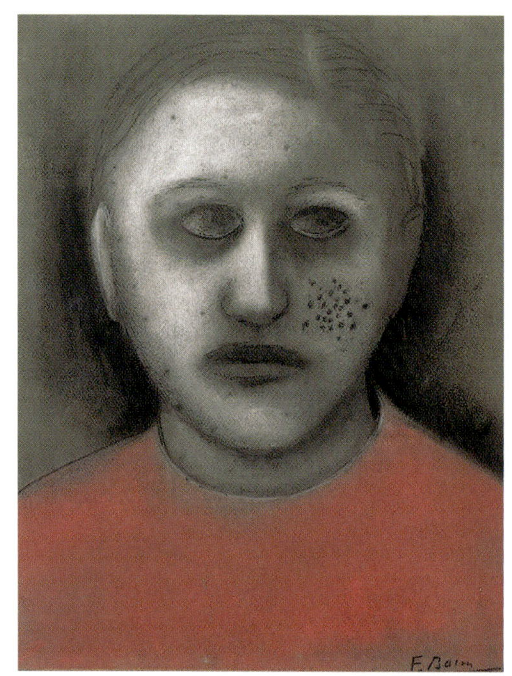

1 │ PORTRAIT *c*.1931–2

Pastel on paper · 40 × 32cm
Private collection

Early Heads *c.*1931–53

Bacon began working as an artist after seeing an exhibition of Picasso's drawings in 1927. *Portrait* (1), the earliest work here and the first documented head, dates from the first decade of Bacon's career, when his activity as a painter was intermittent and characterised by the self-critical destruction of much of his work. The portrait was done from Bacon's imagination and shows the influence of the surrealist painter Pavel Tchelitchew.

In late 1949 Bacon had his first solo show at the Hanover Gallery in London where he showed six studies of heads numbered I to VI. The first, third and last in the series are included here. Following the shocking imagery of his *Three Studies for Figures at the Base of a Crucifixion* 1944 (fig.1), Bacon emphasises man's bestial side in these paintings of the mid-to-late forties. *Head I* (2) resembles a chained or hanged animal screeching in pain; it was included in the exhibition *Wonder and Horror of the Human Head*, organised by Roland Penrose and Lee Miller, at the ICA in London in 1953. From *Head III* (3) onwards, the figure is more obviously human, though there are still undertones of suffering and entrapment. *Head VI* (4) is the first painting in which Bacon combines the image of a gaping mouth with the papal robes and throne derived from Velázquez's portrait of *Pope Innocent X* (fig.2).

The wide-open mouth was based on multiple sources including stills from Eisenstein's film *Battleship Potemkin*, an illustrated book on diseases of the mouth that Bacon had bought in Paris, and the portrayal of a deeply distressed woman in Poussin's *The Massacre of the Innocents*. *Study of a Head* (5) is an almost literal transcription of the close-up of the screaming nursemaid – spectacles smashed, blood running down her cheeks – from the Odessa Steps sequence in *Battleship Potemkin*, which Bacon knew from Roger Manvell's book *Film* (1944). Other critics have linked Bacon's interest in the mouth to the ideas of Bataille and Freud. Bacon himself told David Sylvester: 'I have always been very moved by the movement of the mouth and the teeth. People say that these have all sorts of sexual implications'.

With the exception of *Portrait* and *Head I*, all these early works are painted on the coarse, unprimed side of the canvas – a practice which Bacon never subsequently varied. In *Head VI* and *Study of a Head*, significant areas are left unpainted: it is almost as if an X-ray of the subject had been impressed upon the canvas. The predominantly grey palette, mixed with what appears to be dirt or dust, in *Head I* and *Head III*, and the semi-transparent look of some of the other heads and figures of this period, recall the photographs of ectoplasms and similar psychic apparitions in Baron von Schrenck Notzing's book *Phenomena of Materialisation* (1920), which Bacon owned.

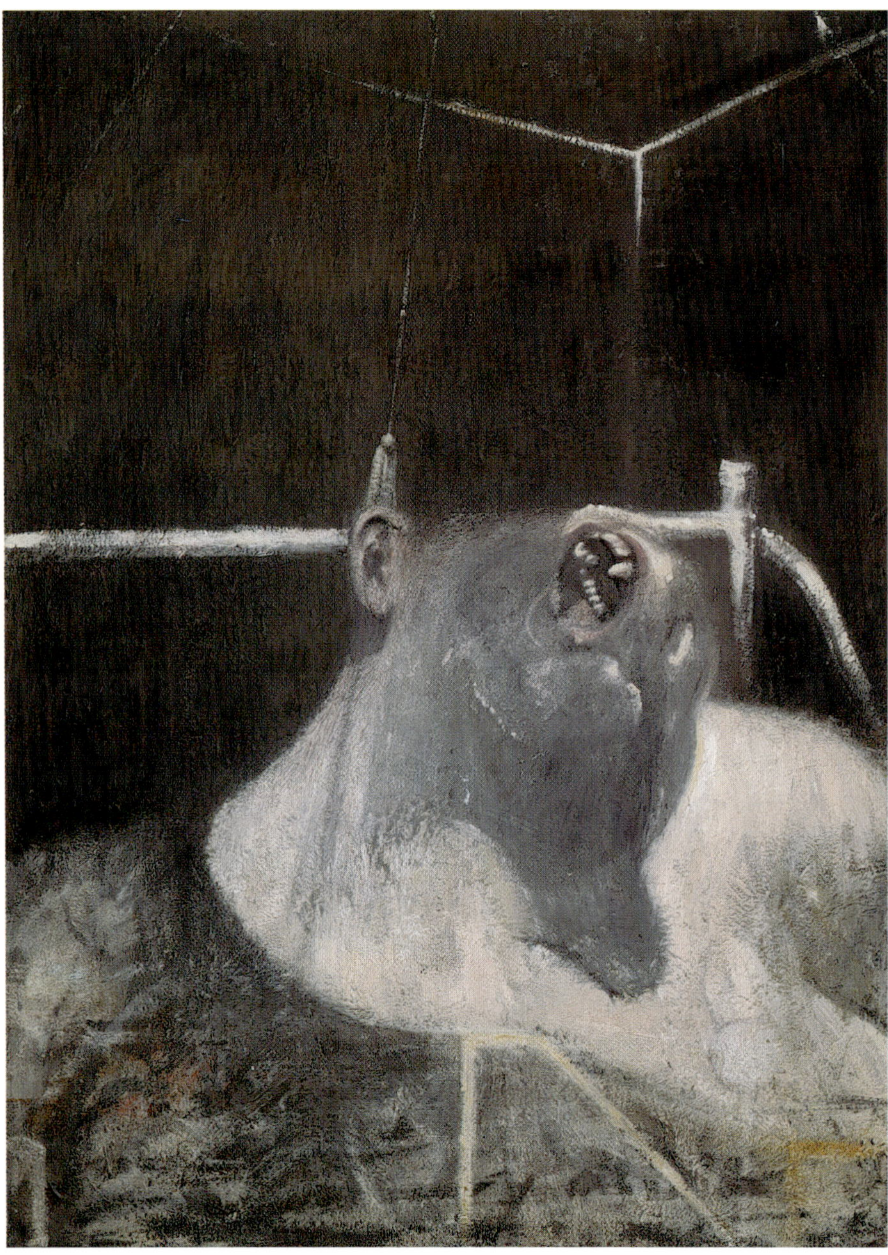

2 | HEAD I, 1948

Oil and tempera on board · 103 × 75cm
Richard S. Zeisler Collection, New York

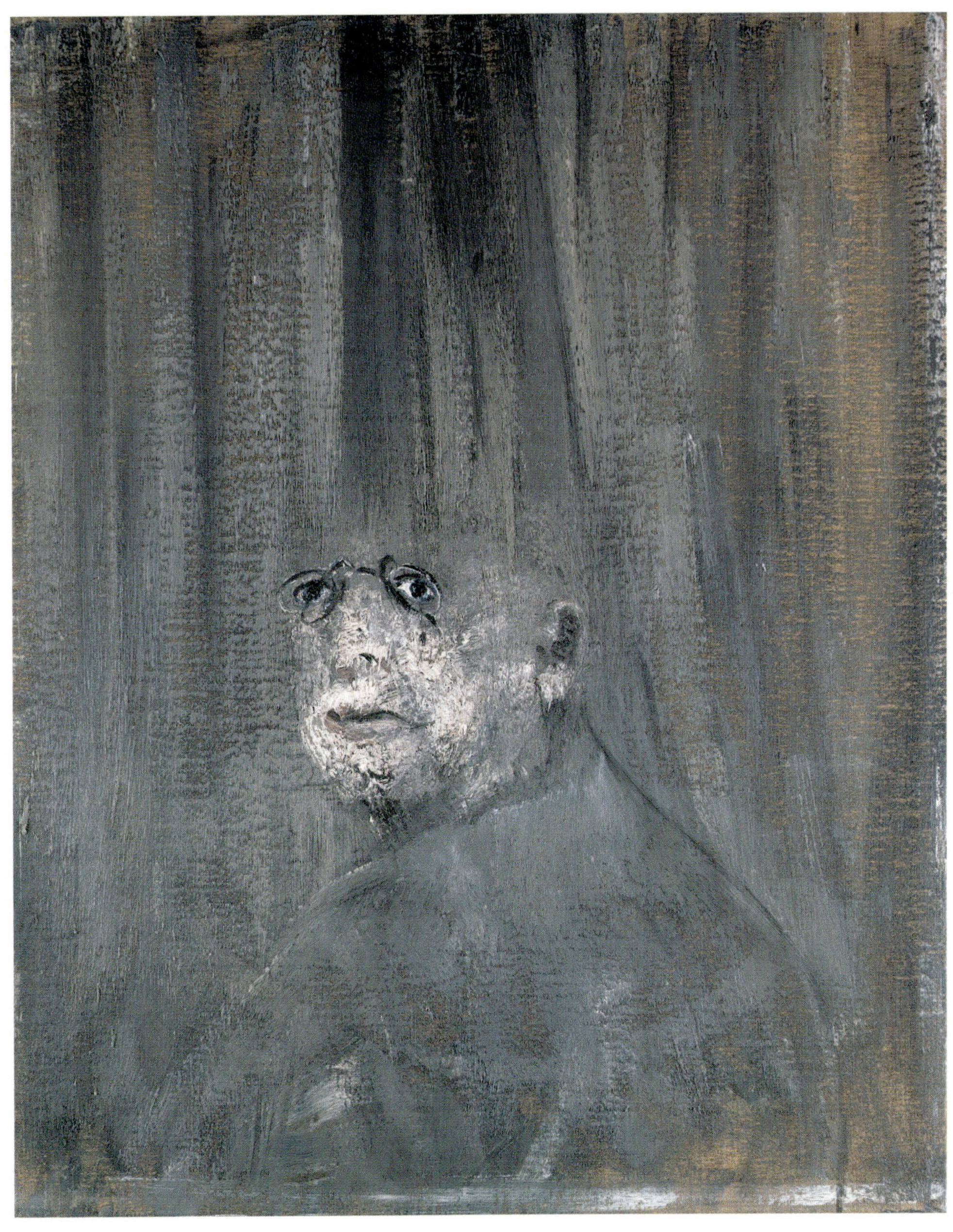

3 | HEAD III, 1949

Oil on canvas · 81 × 66cm
Private collection

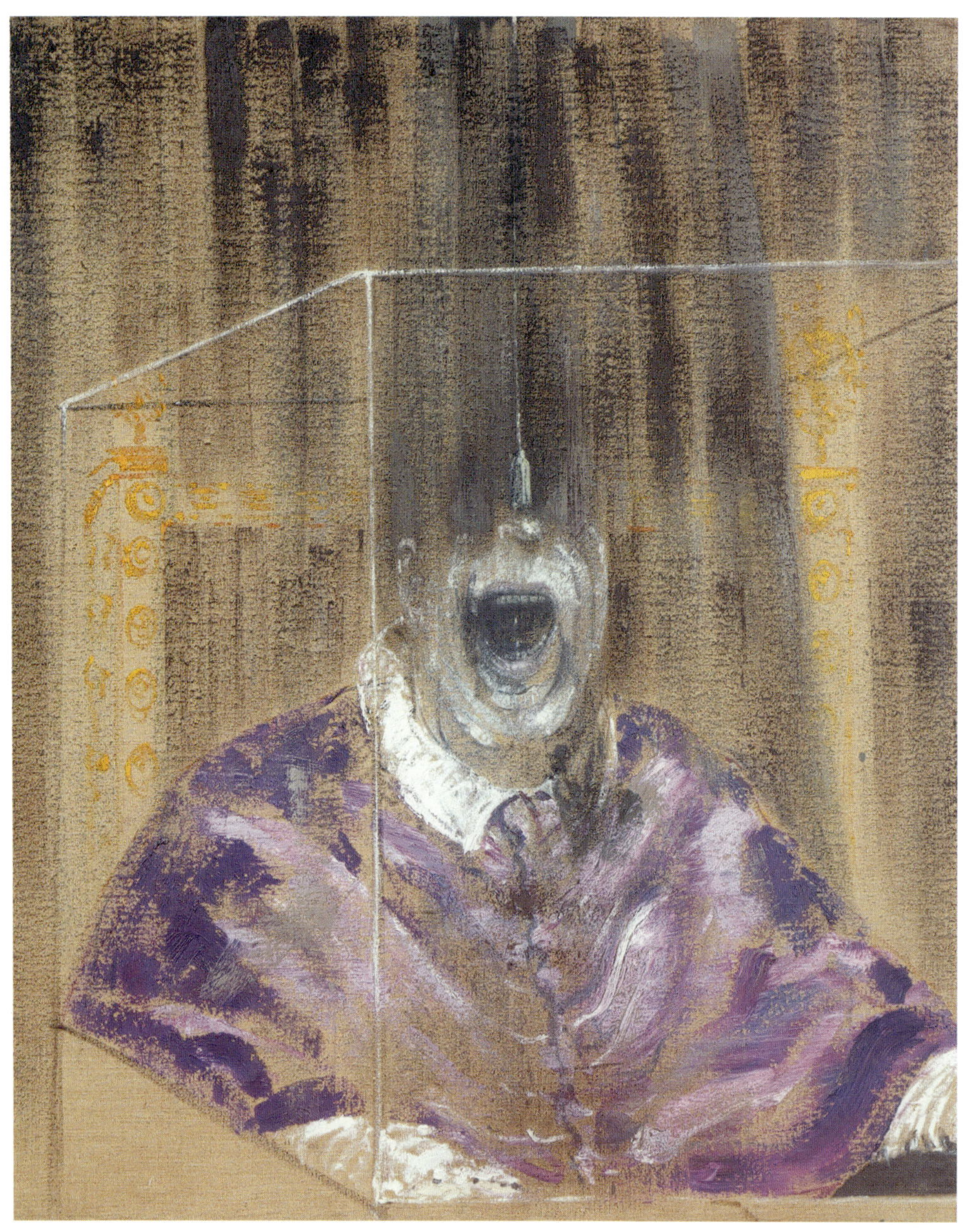

4 | HEAD VI, 1949

Oil on canvas · 93.2 × 76.5cm
Arts Council Collection

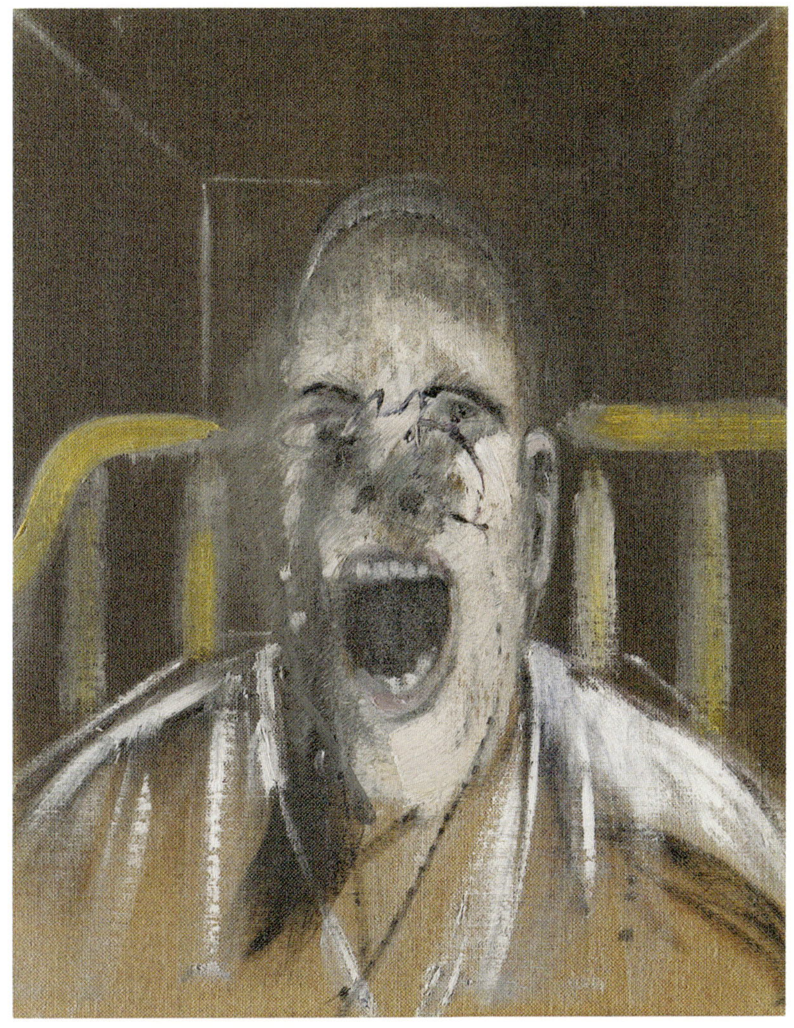

5 | STUDY OF A HEAD, 1952

Oil on canvas · 50 × 40.5cm
Yale Center for British Art, New Haven
Gift of Beekman C. and Margaret H. Cannon

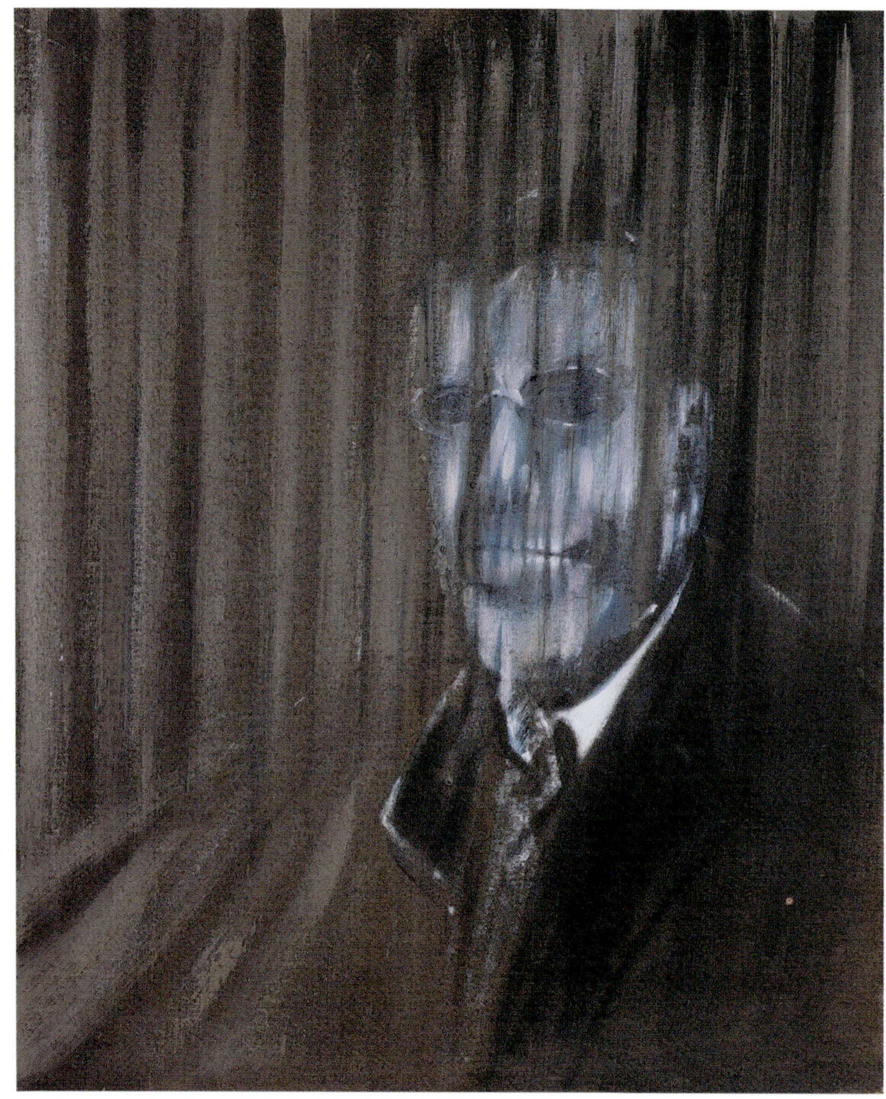

6 | STUDY OF THE HUMAN HEAD, 1953

Oil on canvas · 61 × 51cm
Private collection

Early Portraits 1949–55

Although the inclusion of a linear, transparent enclosure around the figures in *Study for Portrait* (7) and *Portrait of Lucian Freud* (8) might suggest imprisonment of some kind, this was, according to Bacon, a structural device. The artist often used it to isolate and draw attention to the figure. The bedposts and rails in *Study for a Portrait* (9) and *Study for Figure II* (10) function in a similar way. The cage-like frame also appears in some of Giacometti's sculptures – an artist Bacon greatly admired. The vertical streaks or striations in *Study for a Portrait* are another distancing device which Bacon may have based on illustrations of seances in Schrenck Notzing's book.

Portrait of Lucian Freud and *Study for Figure II* contain large areas of canvas that are left unpainted or only very perfunctorily sketched in, and yet the sense of an integrated human form is powerfully conveyed. The paint texture in *Study for Figure II* is thin and dry, thickening only at certain crucial points such as the face, where the features are smudged and blurred. Both pictures employ a highly restricted palette. Although Freud posed for his portrait, when he arrived for the first (of five) sittings, he found that it was almost finished. However, the more Bacon worked on it the less he felt it looked like him and the more it resembled a reproduction of a photograph of Kafka which Bacon had been looking at.

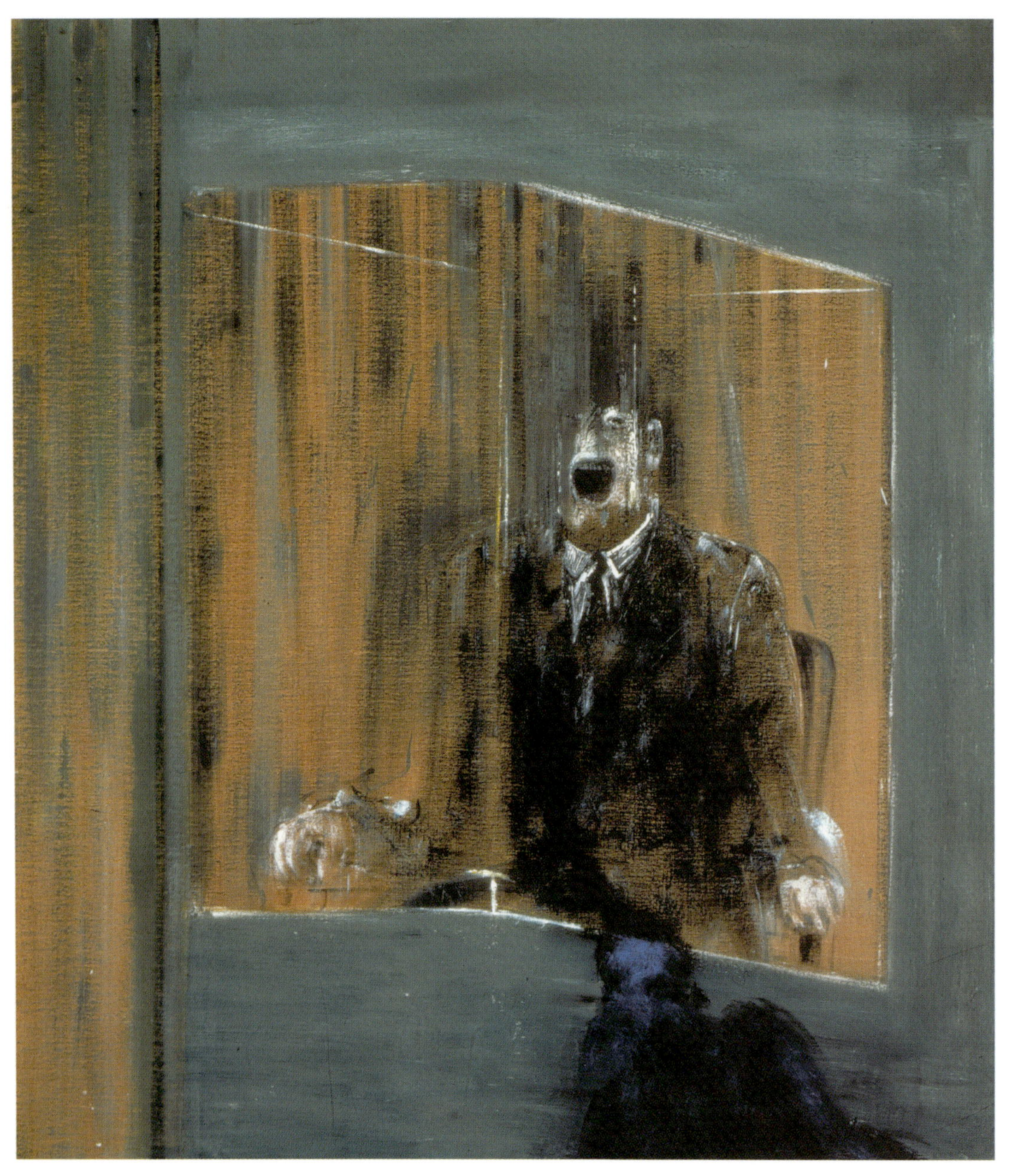

7 | STUDY FOR PORTRAIT, 1949

Oil on canvas · 147.5 × 131cm
Museum of Contemporary Art, Chicago
Gift of Joseph and Jory Shapiro

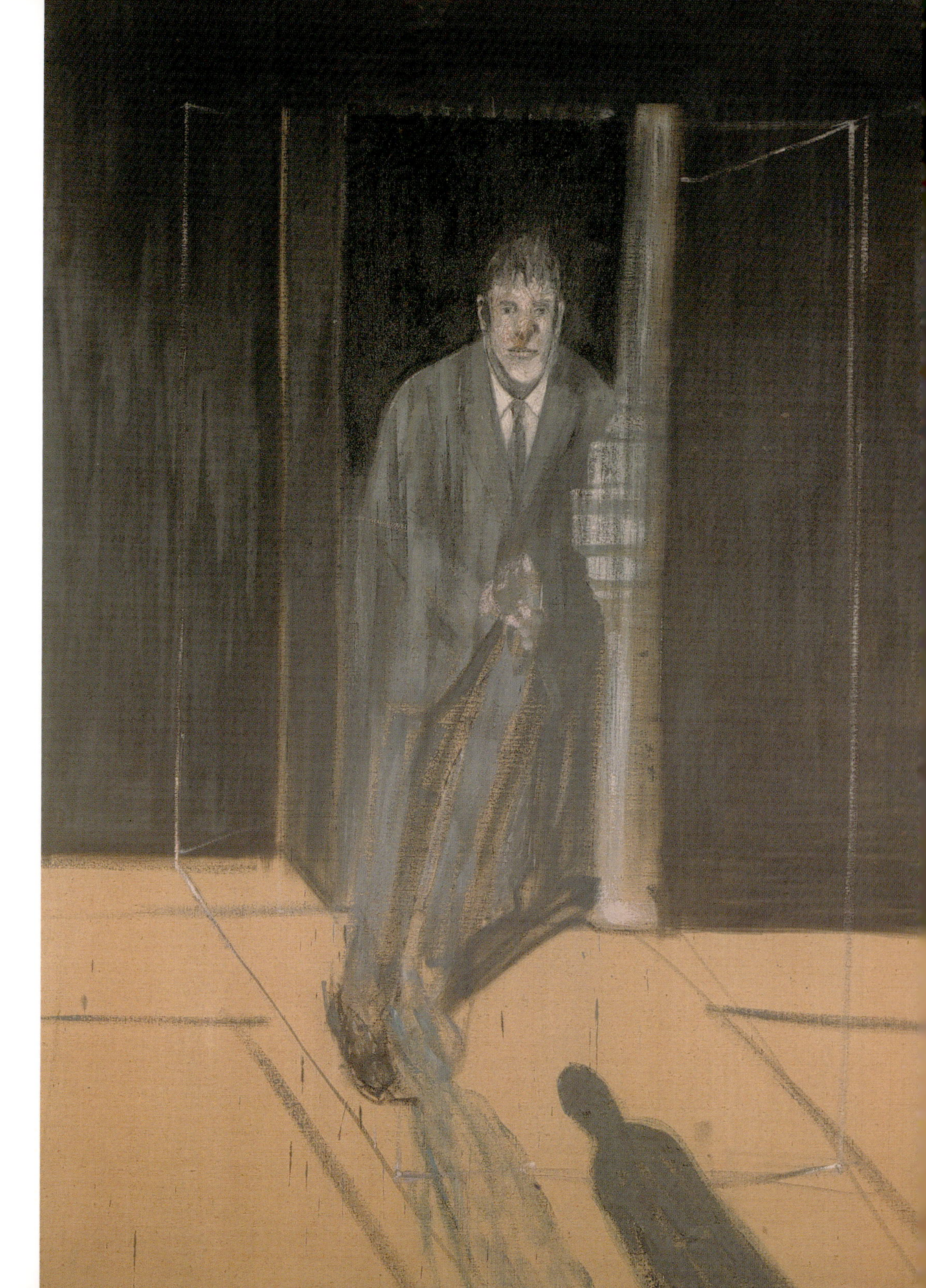

8 | PORTRAIT OF LUCIAN FREUD, 1951

Oil on canvas · 198 × 137cm
The Whitworth Art Gallery, The University
of Manchester

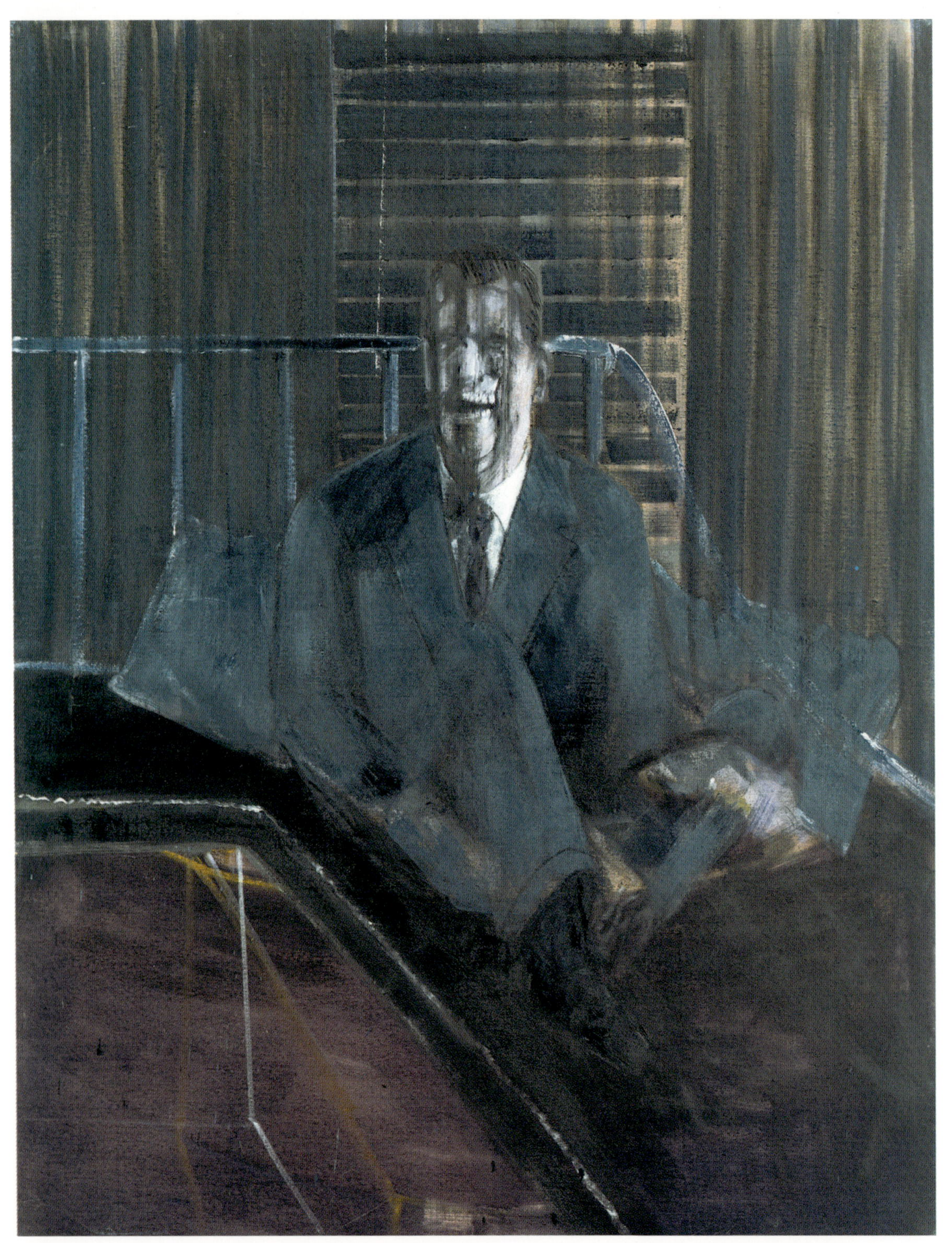

9 | STUDY FOR A PORTRAIT, 1953

Oil on canvas · 152.5 × 118cm
Hamburg Kunsthalle

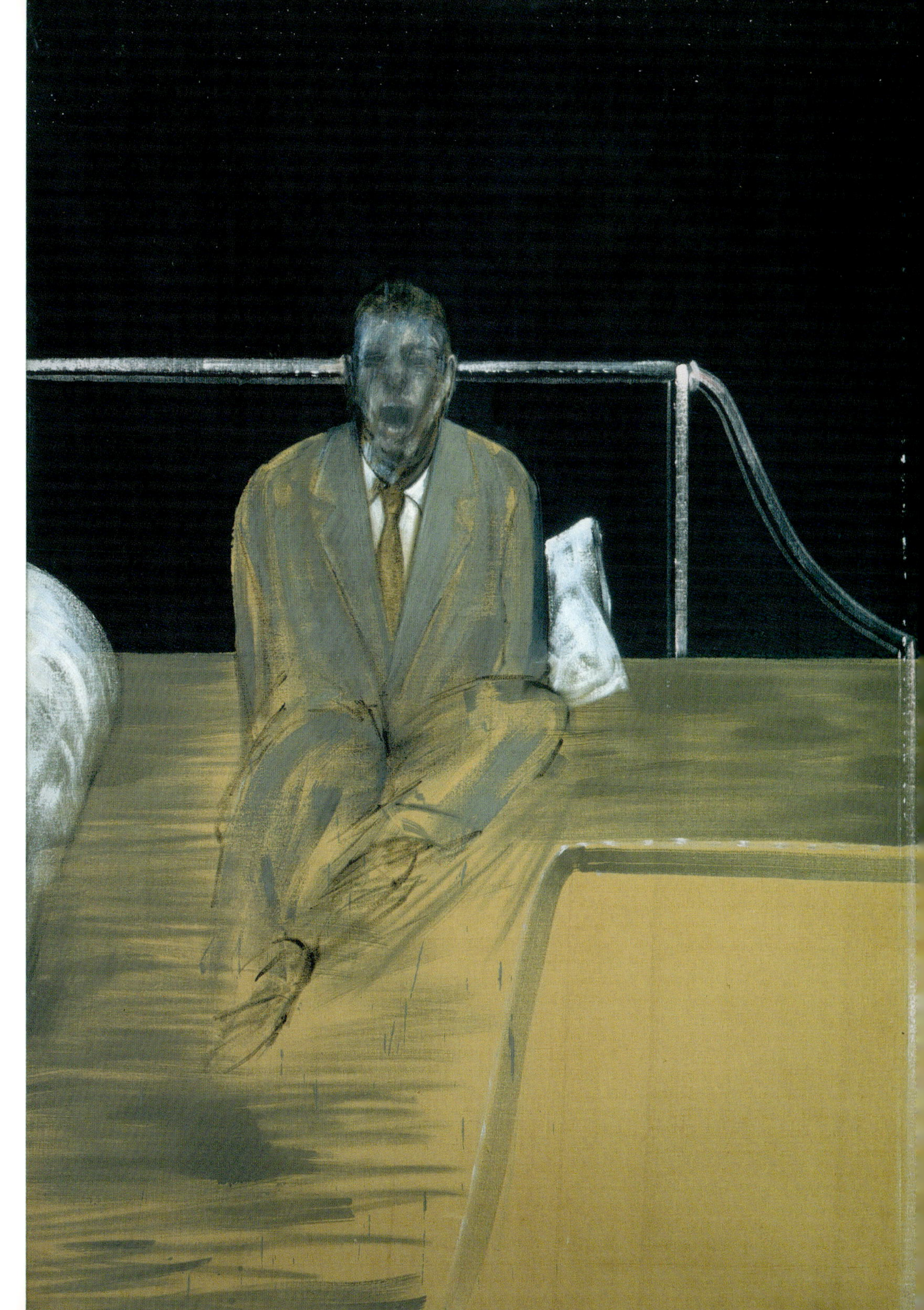

10 | STUDY FOR FIGURE II, 1953/1955

Oil on canvas · 198 × 137cm
Mr and Mrs J. Tomilson Hill

Men in Blue 1954

Bacon painted a total of seven 'Man in Blue' pictures in the spring of 1954; they were exhibited at the Hanover Gallery that summer, numbered I to VII. They were painted partly from a living model, a man Bacon met in a hotel at Henley-on-Thames, and partly from memories of his lover Peter Lacy, who owned a cottage nearby; they may also hint at Bacon's collector-friend Robert Sainsbury, whose wife Lisa was to sit for Bacon the following year. The series is remarkable for its all-over blueness: in terms of tonal range, the pictures are probably the most reductive that Bacon ever painted. Each shows a dark-suited man in an anonymous, claustrophobic interior, perhaps a hotel bar or bedroom, confined by one of the artist's rectangular space frames.

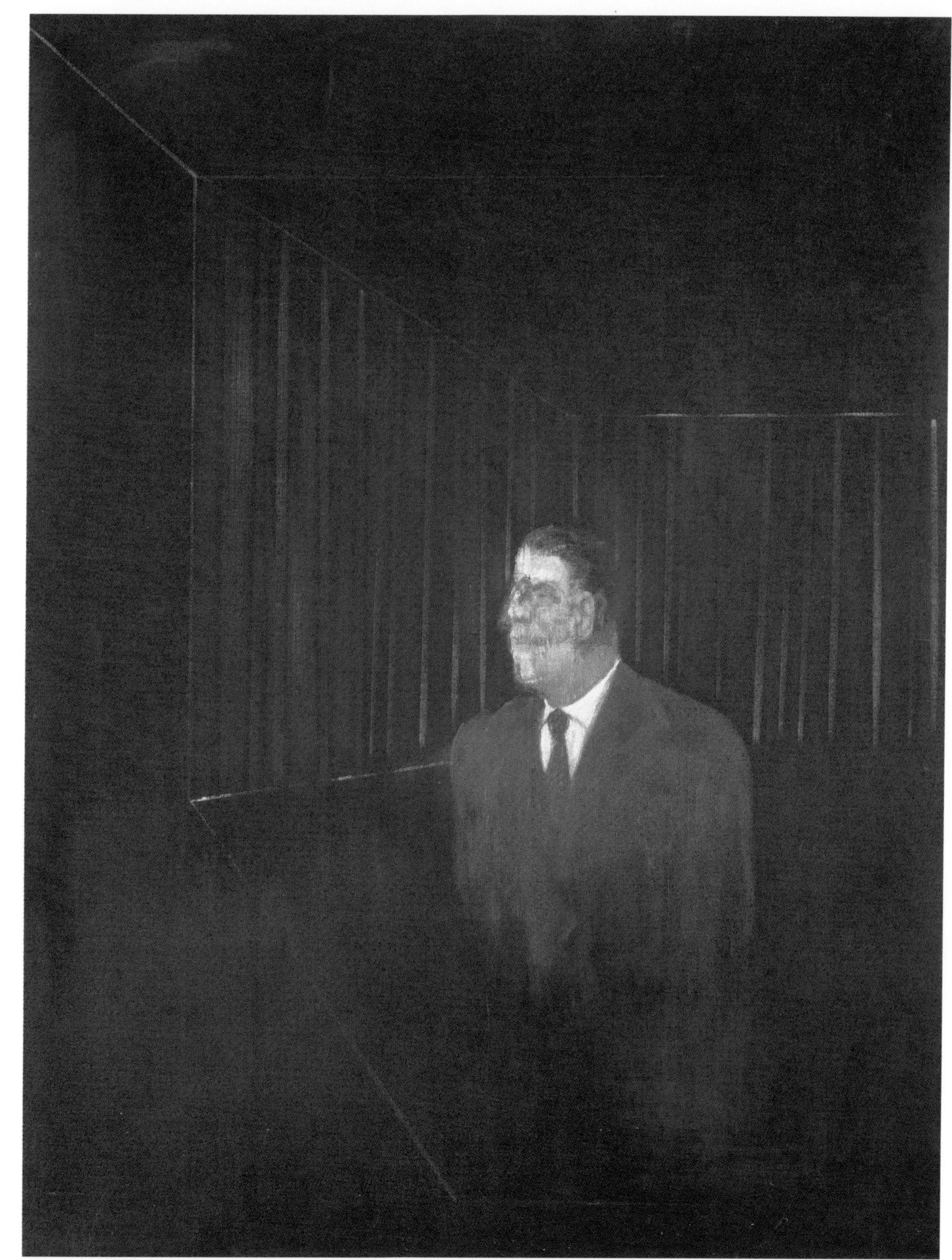

11 | MAN IN BLUE II, 1954

Oil on canvas · 152 × 117cm
Private collection, courtesy Galerie
Beyeler, Basel

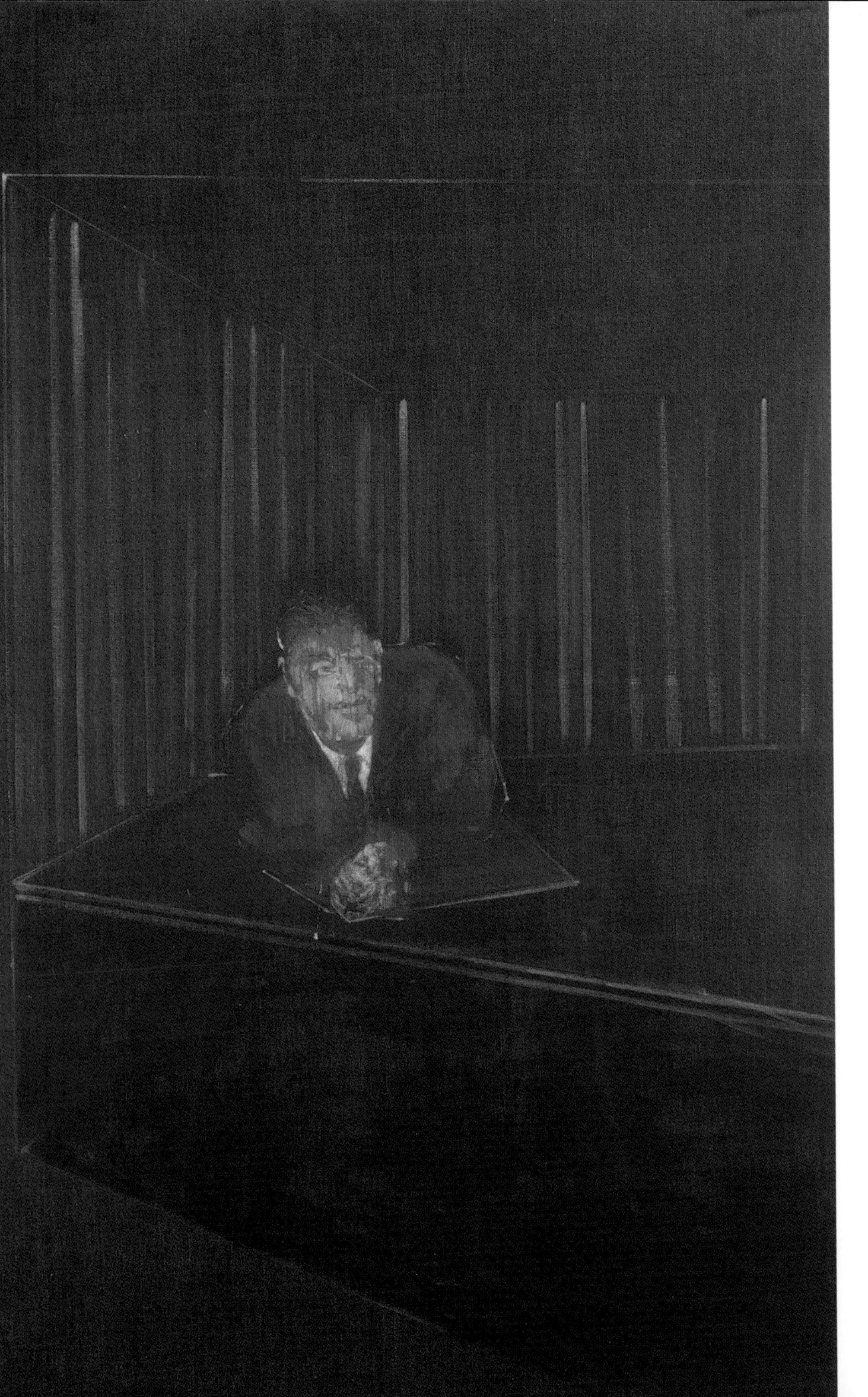

12 | MAN IN BLUE IV, 1954

Oil on canvas · 198 × 137cm
Museum Moderner Kunst, Stiftung Ludwig,
Vienna

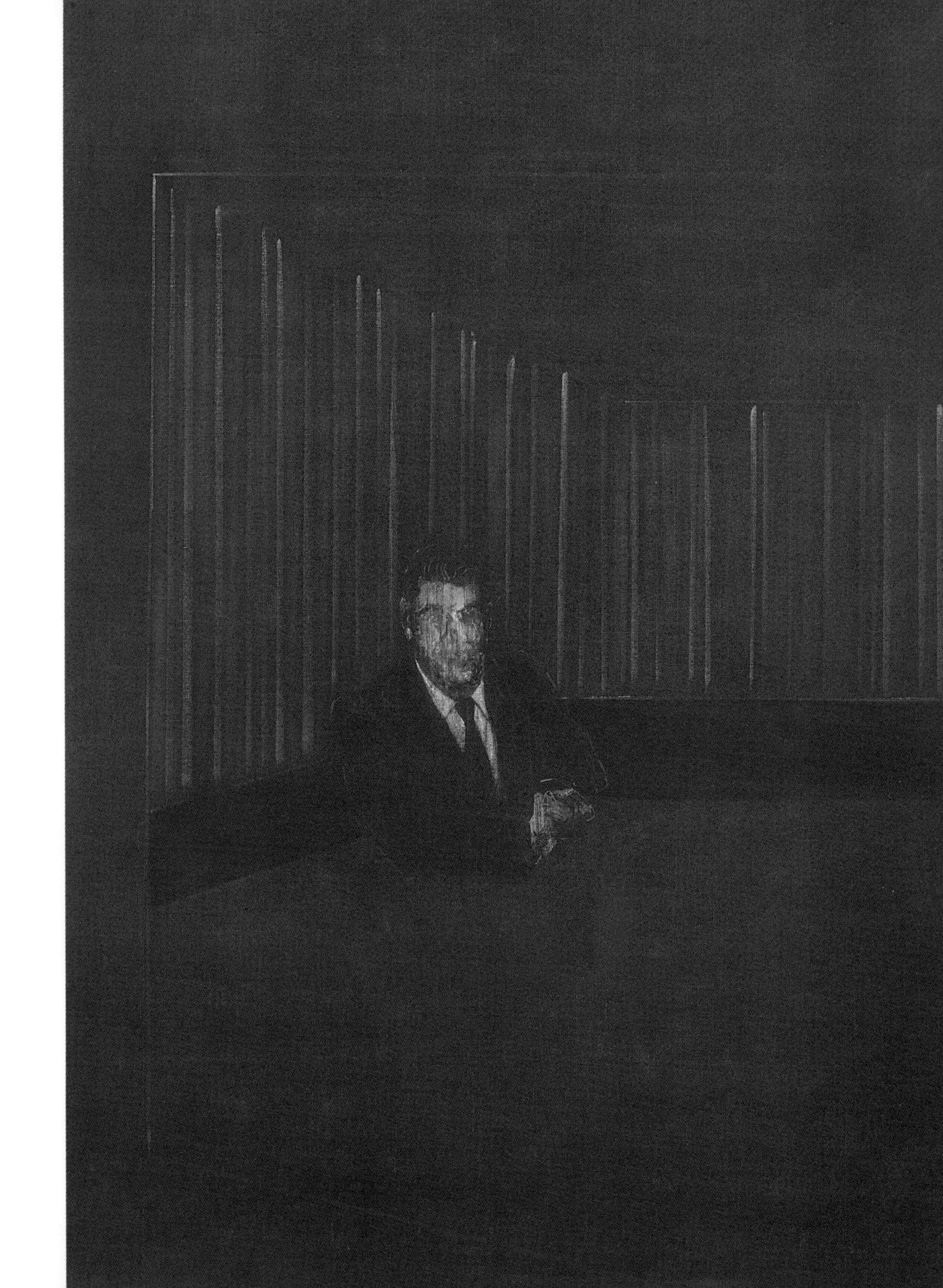

13 | MAN IN BLUE V, 1954

Oil on canvas · 198 × 137cm
Kunstsammlung Nordrhein-Westfalen,
Düsseldorf

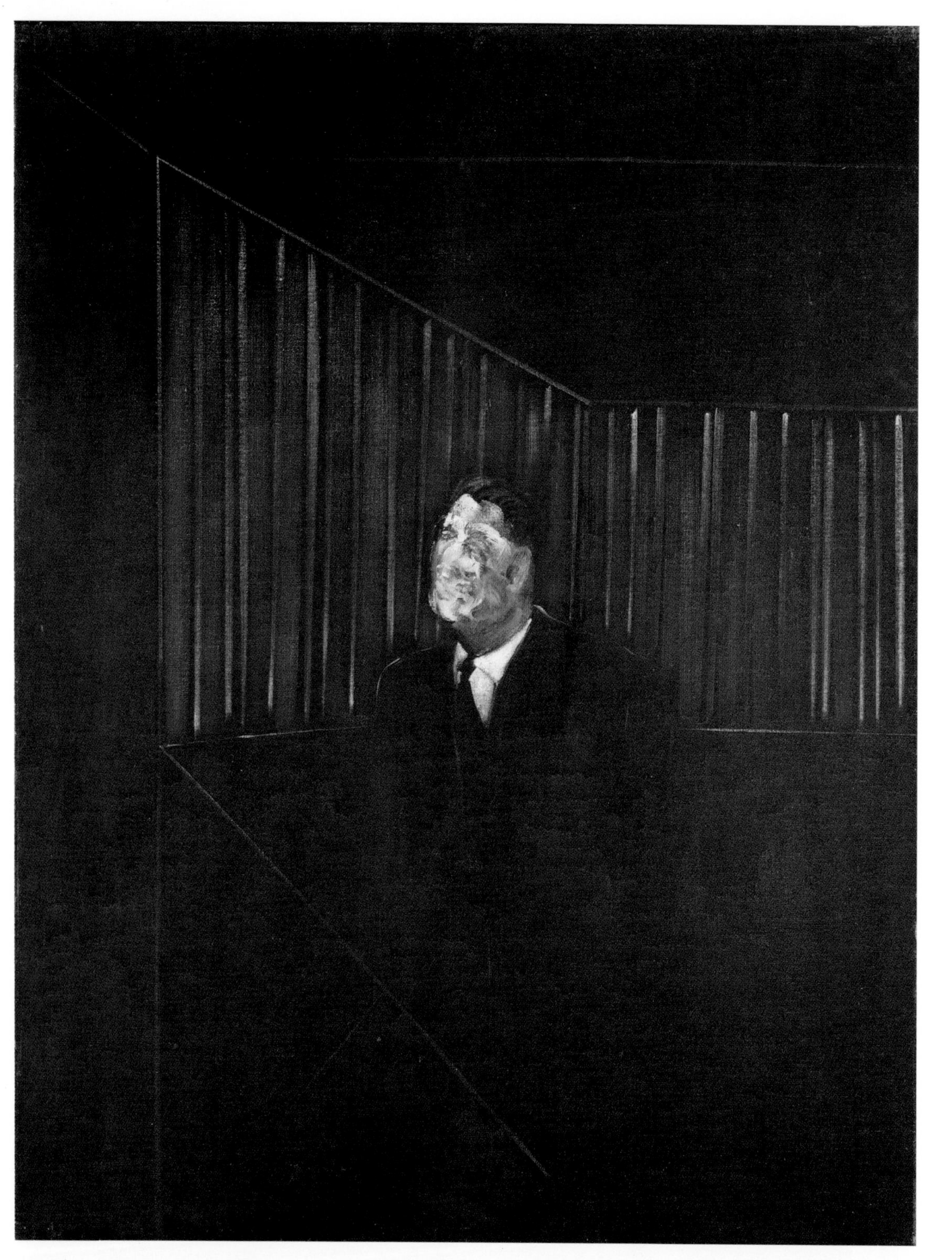

14 | MAN IN BLUE VII, 1954

Oil on canvas · 152.5 × 117cm
Private collection, courtesy Christie's

Portraits and Heads 1955–63

This group of works demonstrates Bacon's growing sophistication in the handling of paint. In 1955–6 Bacon painted a series of four pictures based on a photograph in a book of a plaster cast of the famous life mask of William Blake. The photograph showed the head centrally placed against a dark background, a feature that Bacon retained in his transformations of the image. *Study for Portrait II (after the Life Mask of William Blake)* (15) is arguably the finest in the series, in which the brushstrokes do not simply describe the forms, they *become* the forms: subject and paint are indivisible. This metamorphic process is at the heart of Bacon's work. It can be seen in the increasingly intuitive or improvised way in which subsequent heads seem to materialise on canvas before our eyes: *Head of a Man* (16) and *Head of Man* (17) – a boyfriend of Bacon's, called Ron, whom he had met in a gambling club in Soho; the intensely animated face of *Miss Muriel Belcher* (18), seen in profile against a green background, perhaps the walls of the Colony Room over which she presided; the tender *Head of Boy* (19); and *Portrait of Man with Glasses III* and *IV* (22 & 23). The last two are the most disturbing in a series of four heads, in which the fierce energy of Bacon's brushmarks combines with a sense of physiognomic collapse to create images that vibrate with demonic life. The mysterious *Reclining Man with Sculpture* (20) may be a self-portrait – the raised arm gesture was characteristic of Bacon – though whether the effigy on the table originated in William Redgrave's small bronze bust of Bacon, as Martin Harrison suggests, or alludes more generally to the tradition of antique sculpture which Bacon admired, is unclear.

In 1956–7 Bacon painted eight large pictures inspired by a reproduction of Van Gogh's *The Painter on the Road to Tarascon*. This extended dialogue with the older master affected his art in two ways. First, Bacon's palette shifted into a higher key, with passages, sometimes great sweeps, of pure bright colour now prominent. And second, his painted forms were increasingly made up of non-rational – what Bacon would have called 'non-illustrational' – marks and textures, applied with a variety of objects as well as with the brush.

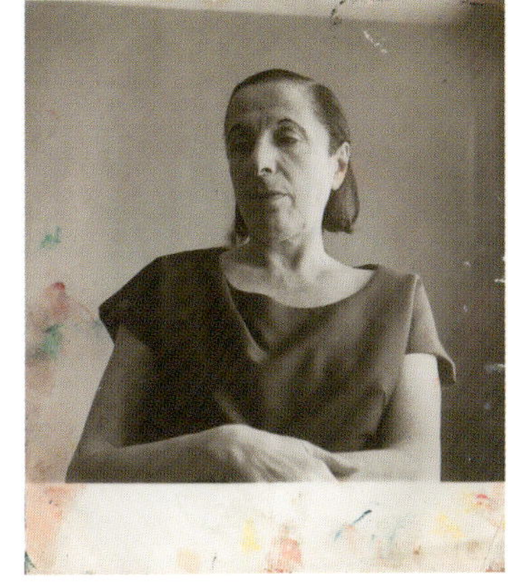

John Deakin *Muriel Belcher, c.*1964
Dublin City Gallery The Hugh Lane

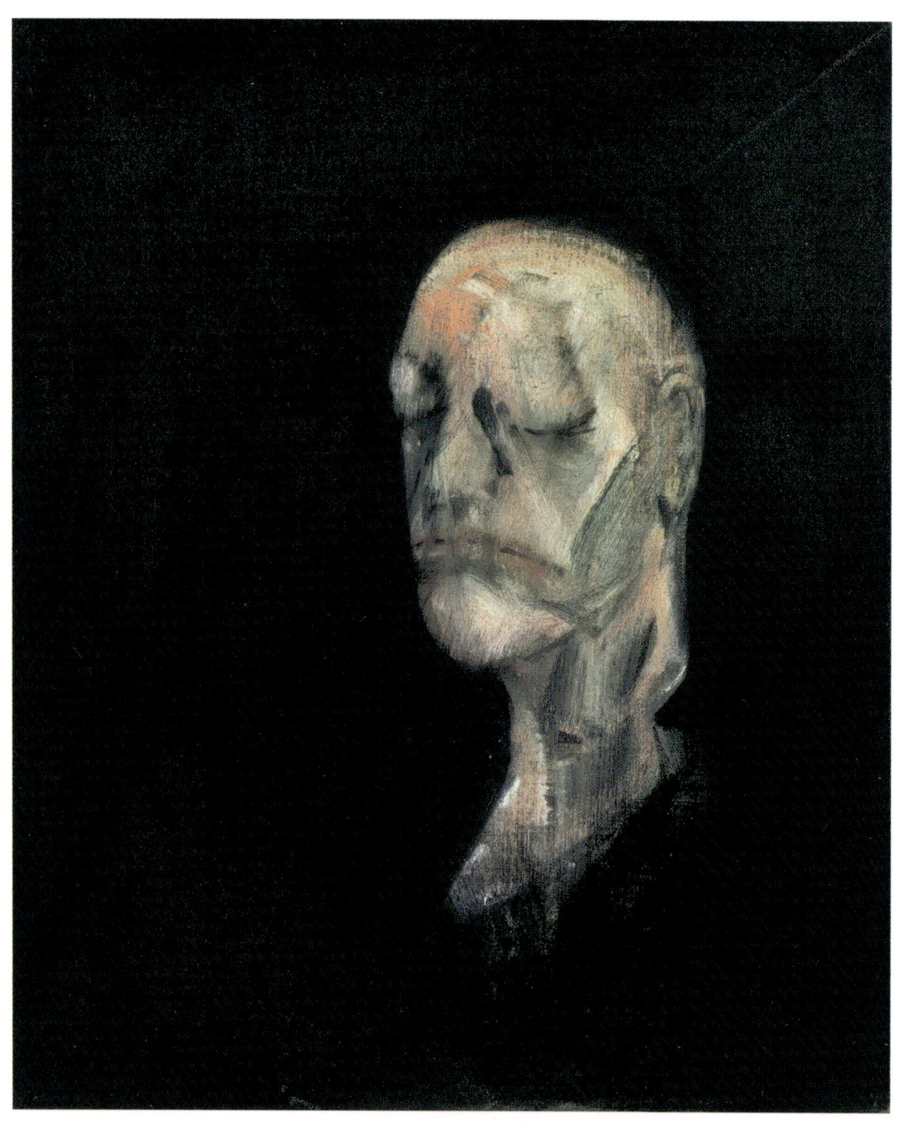

15 | STUDY FOR PORTRAIT II (AFTER THE LIFE MASK OF WILLIAM BLAKE), 1955

Oil on canvas · 61 × 50.8cm
Tate. Purchased 1979

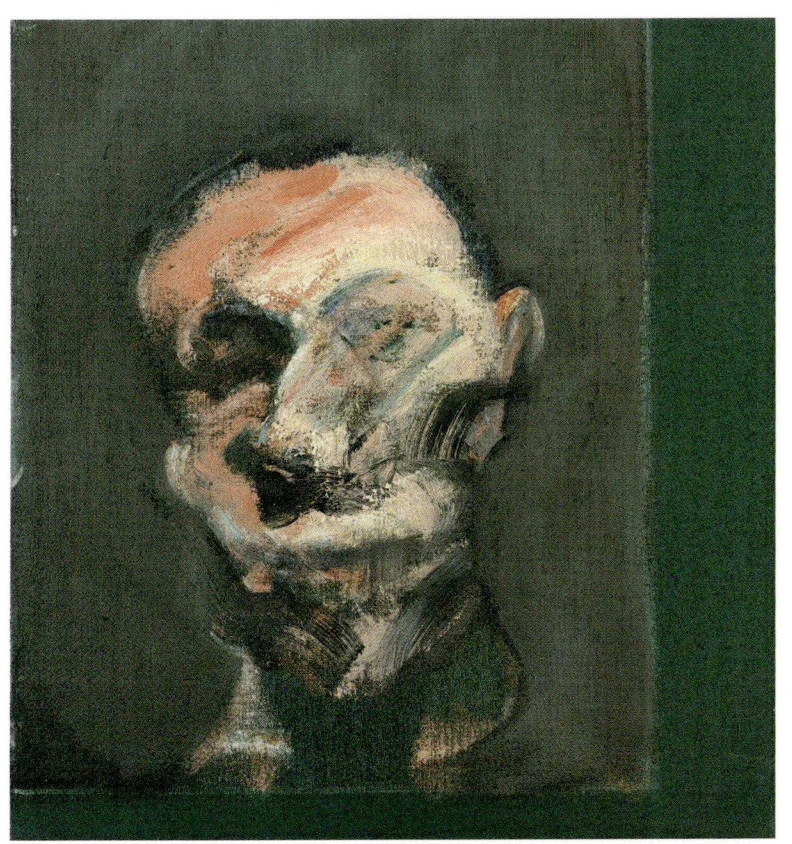

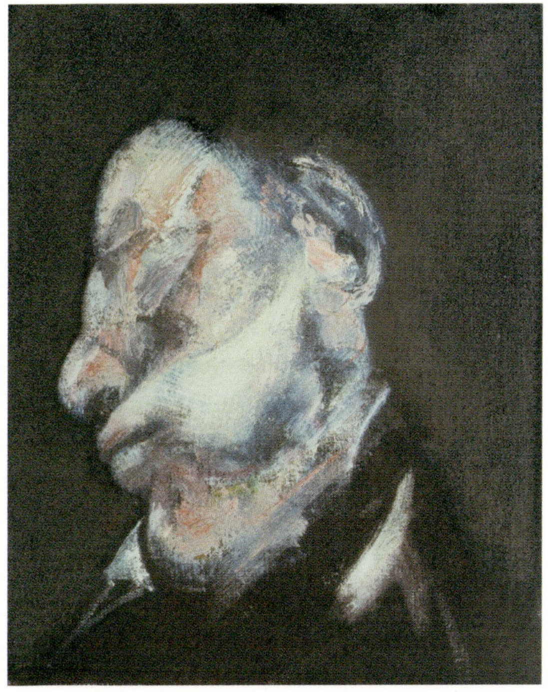

16 | HEAD OF A MAN, 1959

Oil on canvas · 48 × 46.5cm

Private collection

17 | HEAD OF MAN, 1959

Oil on canvas · 34.5 × 28cm

Private collection

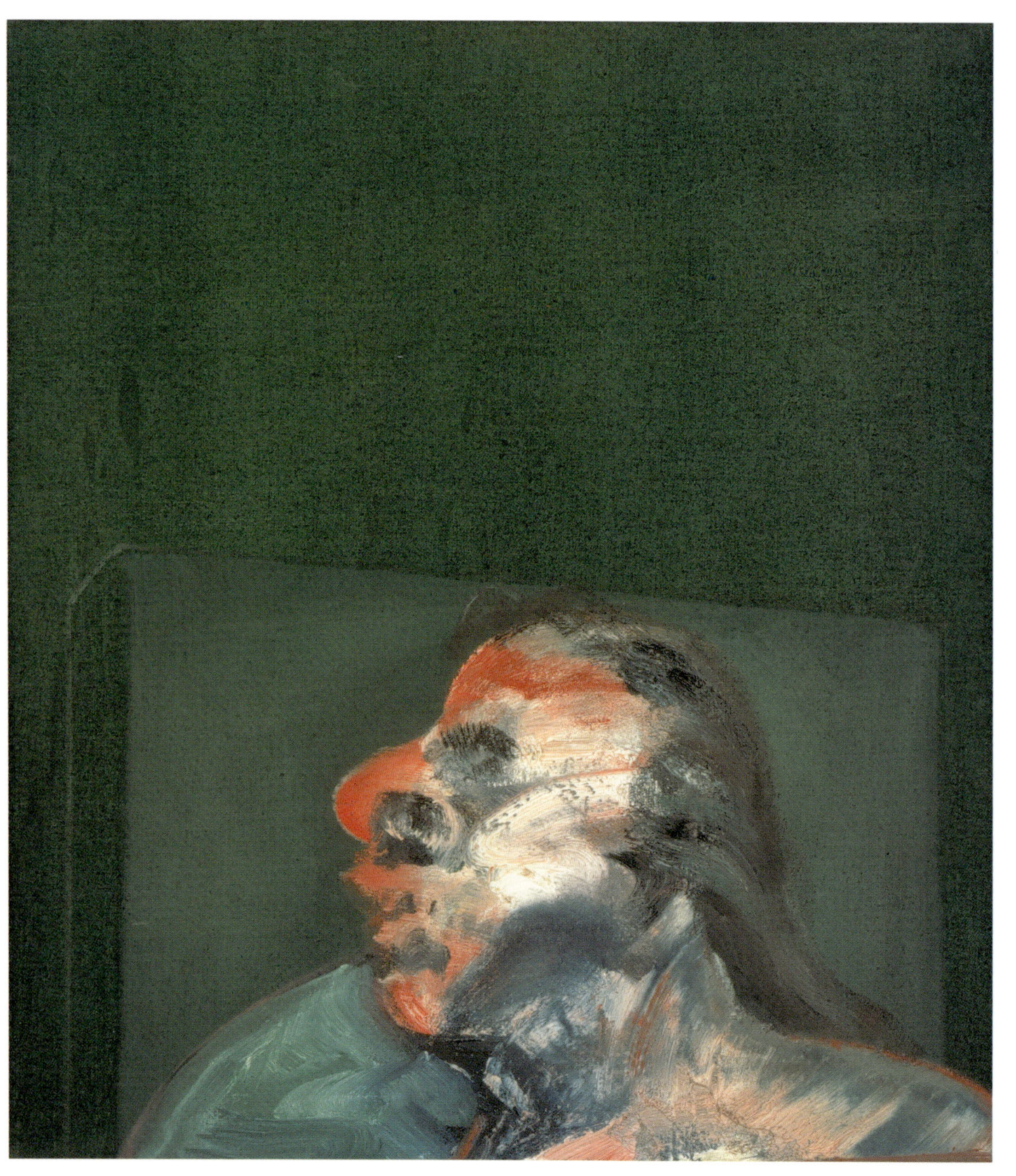

18 | MISS MURIEL BELCHER, 1959

Oil on canvas · 74 × 67.5cm
Private collection

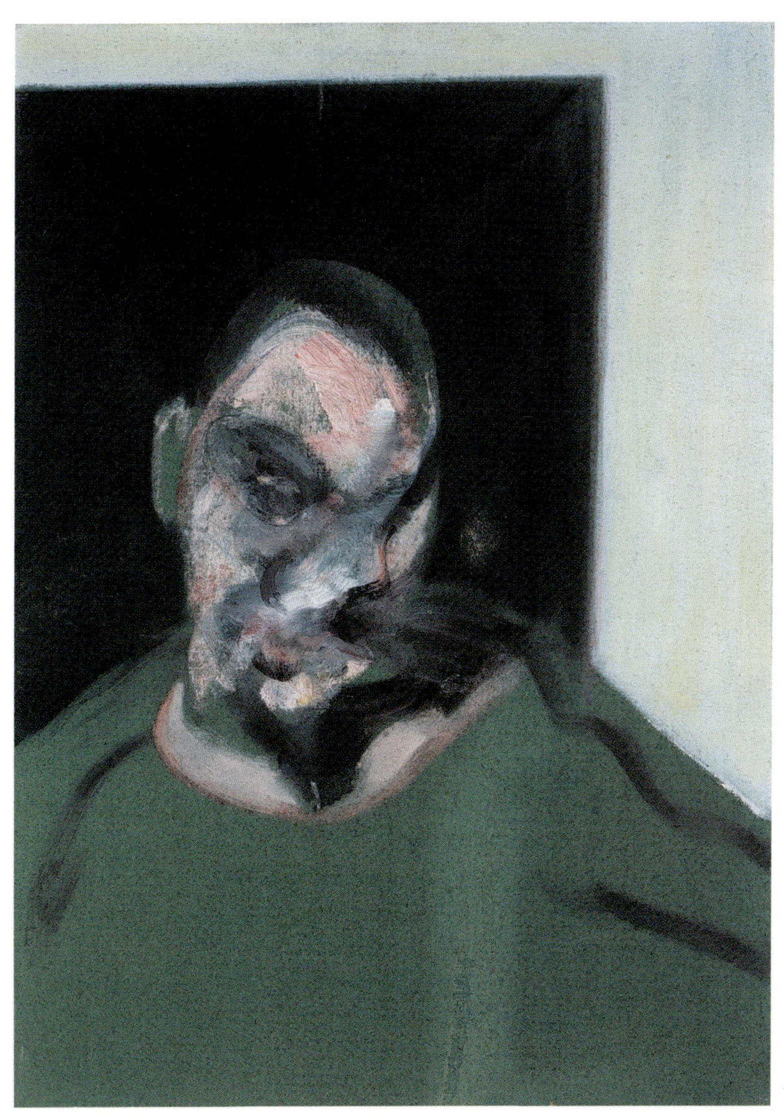

19 │ HEAD OF BOY, 1960

Oil on canvas · 61 × 44.5cm
Private collection

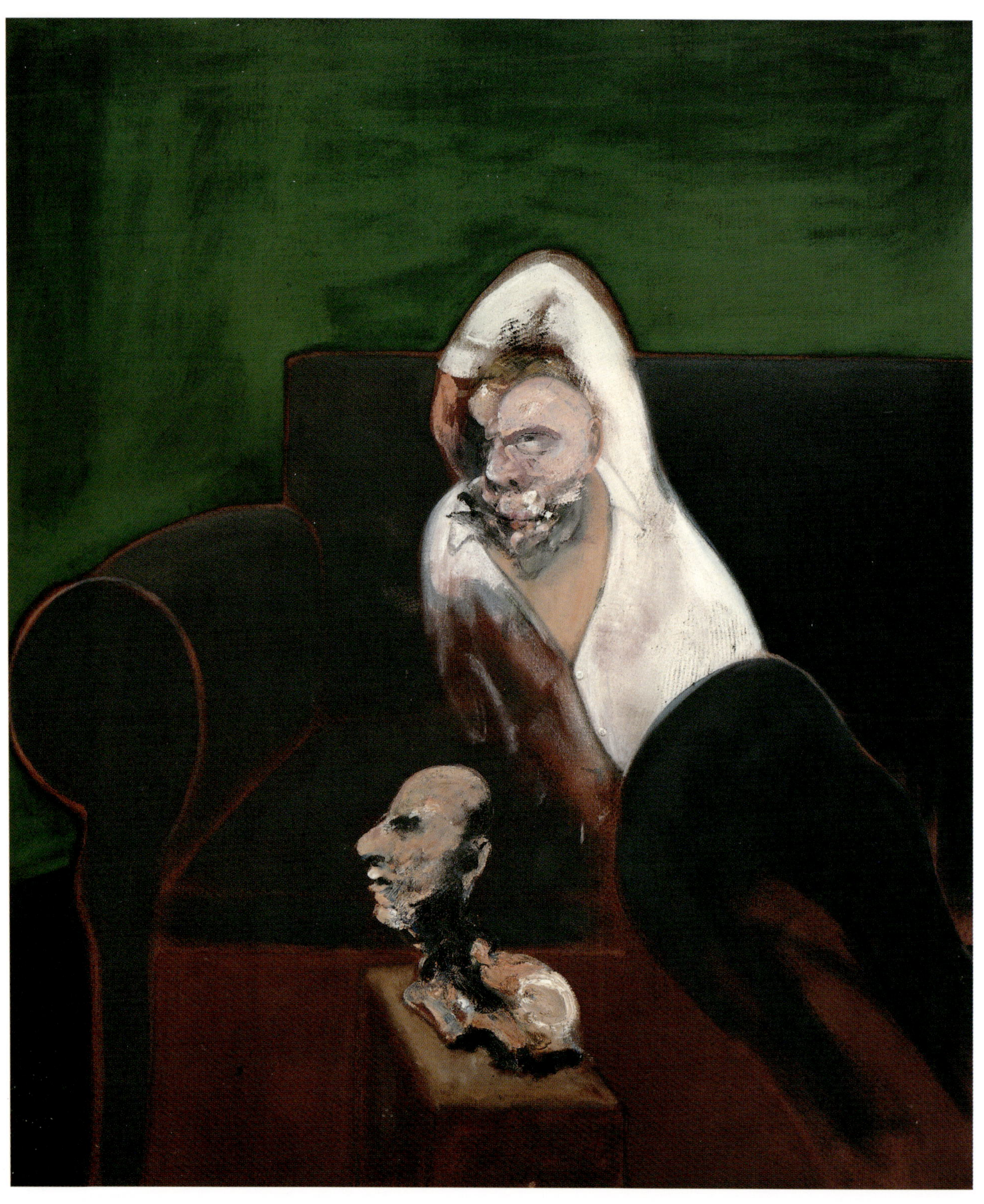

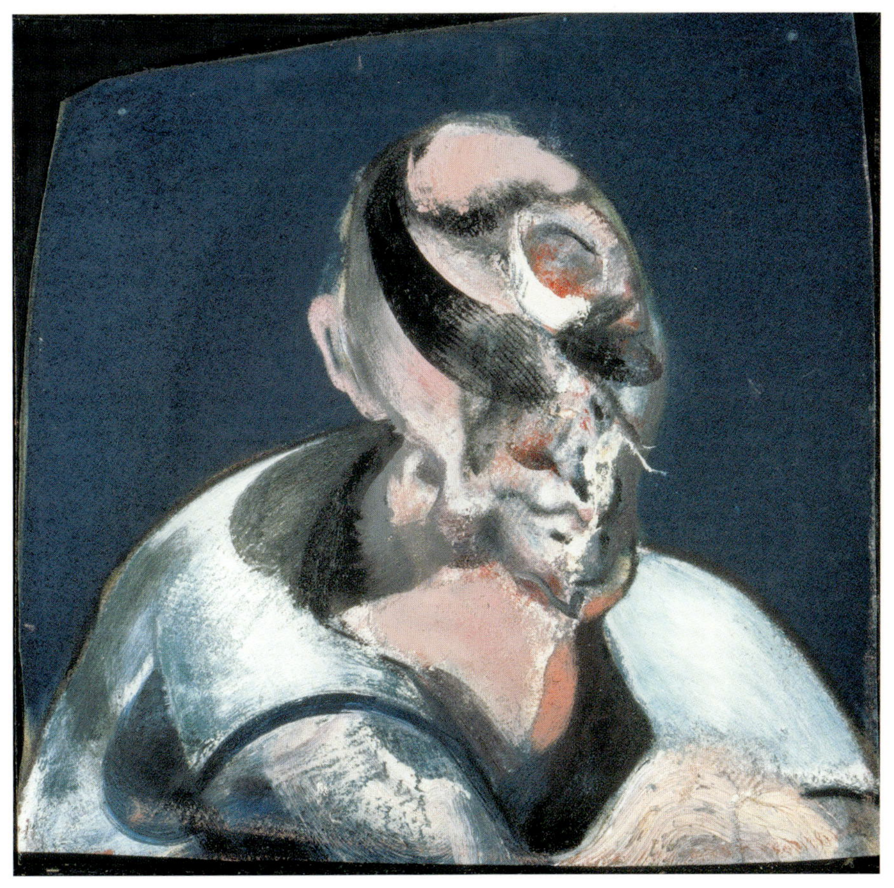

20 | RECLINING MAN WITH SCULPTURE, 1960–1

Oil on canvas · 166.5 × 142cm

Tehran Museum of Contemporary Art

21 | HEAD, 1962

Oil on canvas · 41 × 42.5cm

Private collection

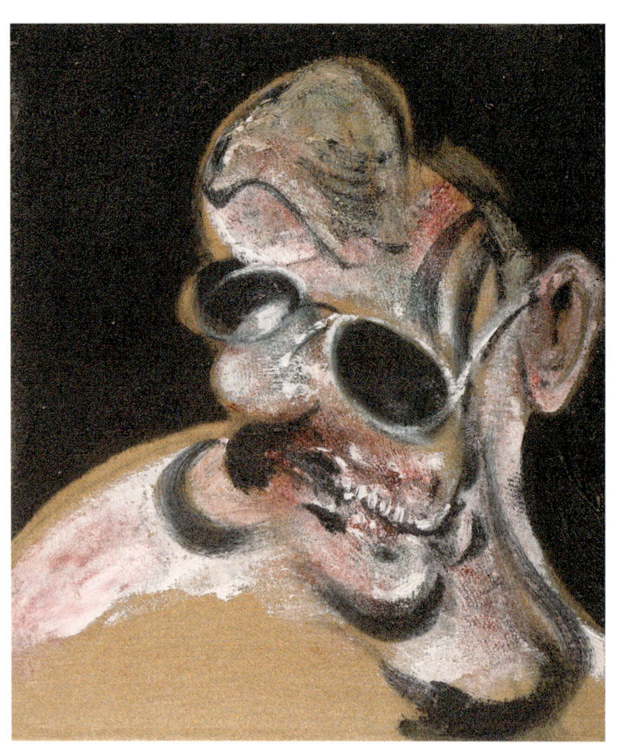

22 | PORTRAIT OF MAN WITH GLASSES III, 1963

Oil on canvas · 33.7 × 28.7cm
Private collection, courtesy Ivor Braka Ltd, London

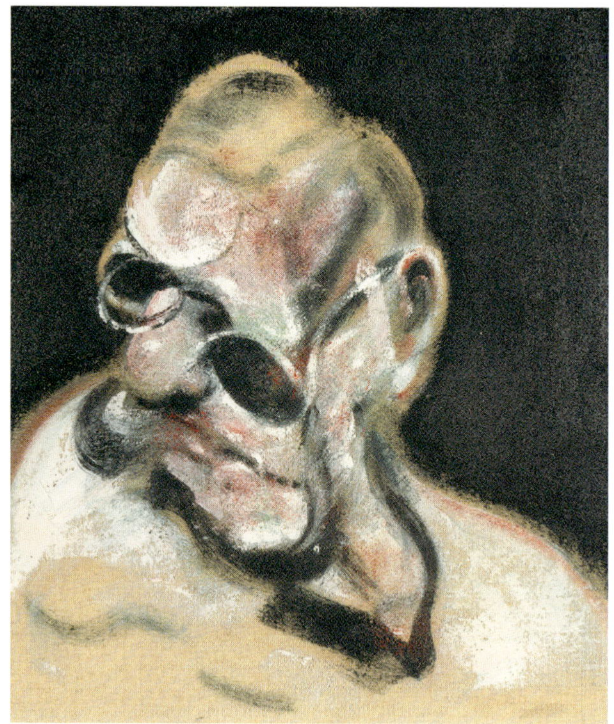

23 | PORTRAIT OF MAN WITH GLASSES IV, 1963

Oil on canvas · 33.7 × 28.7cm
Private collection

Peter Lacy 1955–62

Bacon met Peter Lacy, a former Battle of Britain pilot, in the early 1950s. Their love affair, though often stormy, lasted for a decade. When Lacy went to live in Tangier in the mid-1950s, Bacon would visit him for long periods.

Lacy's image dominated Bacon's painting in the 1950s. This section brings together five works disclosing different aspects, not only of Lacy's personality, but also of his relationship with Bacon. *Head in Grey* (24), painted from memory, shows the artist recalling Lacy's striking features – the lines under the slightly protruding eyes, the swept-back fair hair – with rapid, exploratory strokes. The two reclining figures (25 & 26), one clothed, the other naked, reveal a tender, intimate side to Bacon's art that is absent from his more violent or explicit treatment of physical encounters: they are about love rather than sex. *Sleeping Figure* (26), in particular, confirms the intensity of the relationship: Lacy's body is shown exposed and vulnerable but at the same time Bacon hints at its erotic possibilities.

Head III (27) is one of four close-up studies of Peter Lacy on a black ground that Bacon made in 1961. They were the first to be painted on a canvas measuring approximately 14 × 12 inches, the format Bacon would use for his small heads from now until the end of his life. In *Head III* Bacon's energetic manipulation of paint holds in balance contrasting ideas of movement and repose, of a watchful and at the same time contemplative Lacy.

The final work in this section (28) was painted after Bacon learned of Lacy's alcohol-related death in Tangier, on the day of the opening of his retrospective at the Tate Gallery in 1962. The first of some forty or so small triptychs of heads that Bacon was to paint, it shows three-quarter views of the left and right sides of Lacy's face flanking a view of Bacon full-face. Paradoxically, it is the deathly pale self-portrait in the centre that seems to be dissolving or disappearing, while the two heads of Lacy, however marmoreal, still seem to have life in them.

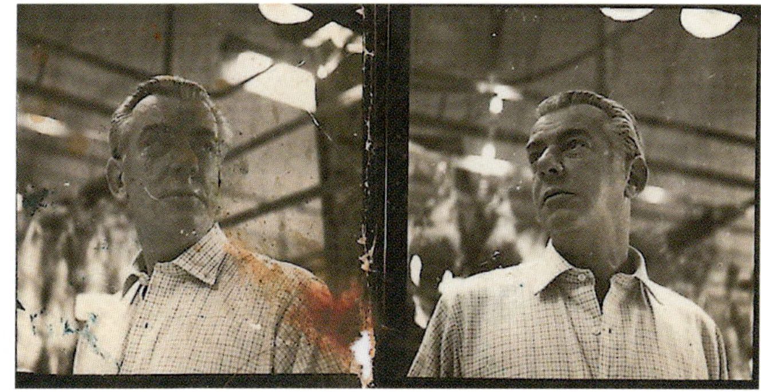

John Deakin *Peter Lacy, c.*1959
Dublin City Gallery The Hugh Lane

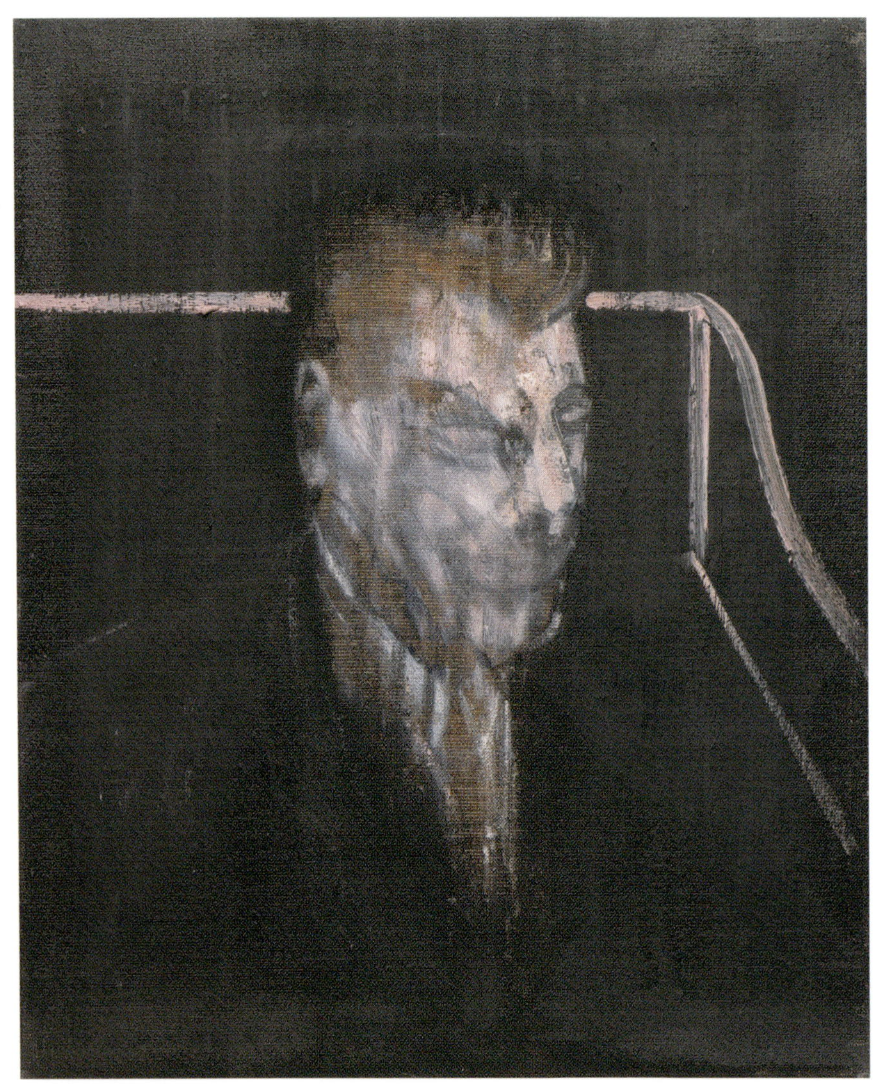

24 | HEAD IN GREY, 1955

Oil on canvas · 61 × 51cm
Walker Art Center, Minneapolis
Gift of Mr and Mrs Edmond R. Ruben, 1995

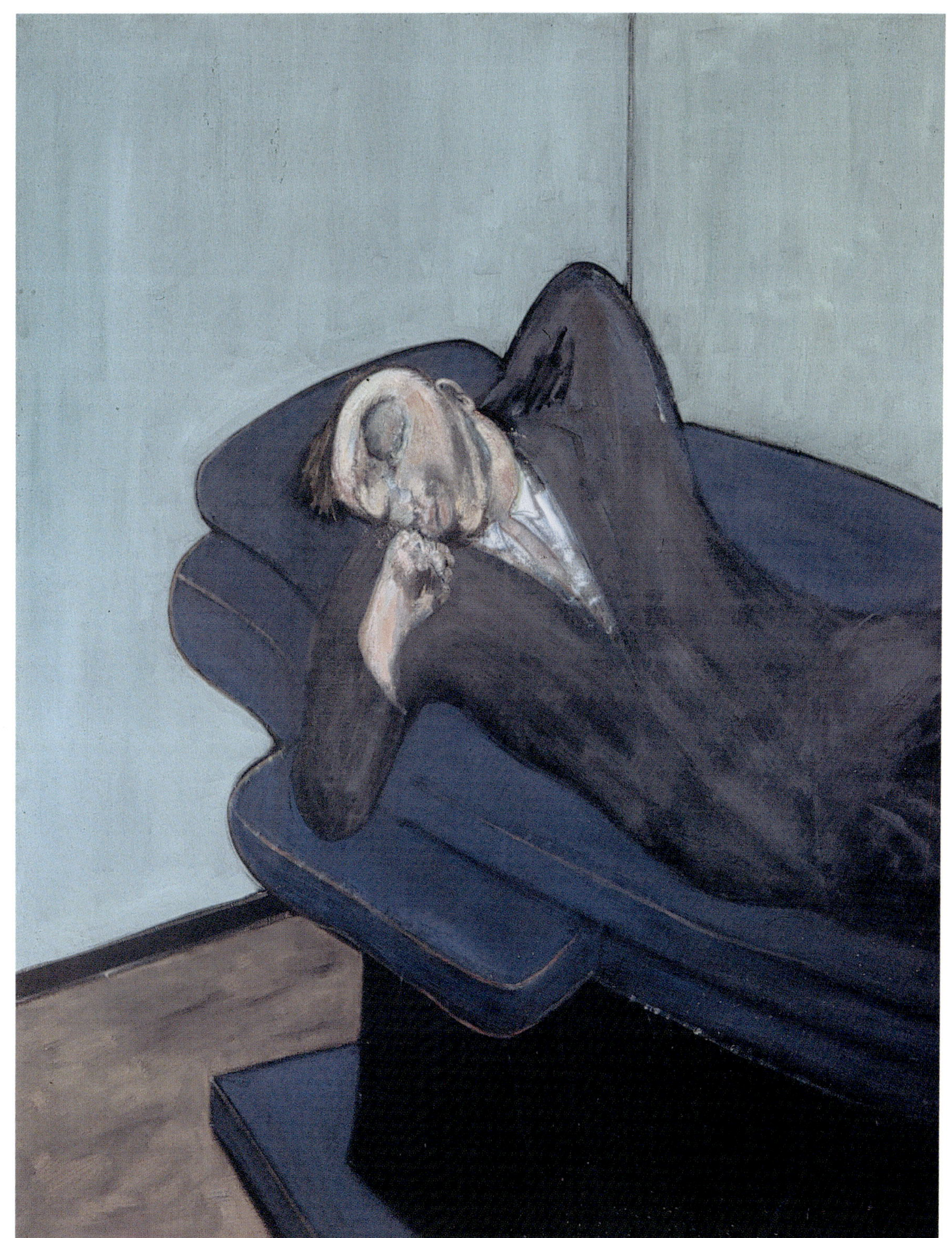

25 | LYING FIGURE, 1958

Oil on canvas · 153.5 × 119.5cm
Museum Bochum, Germany

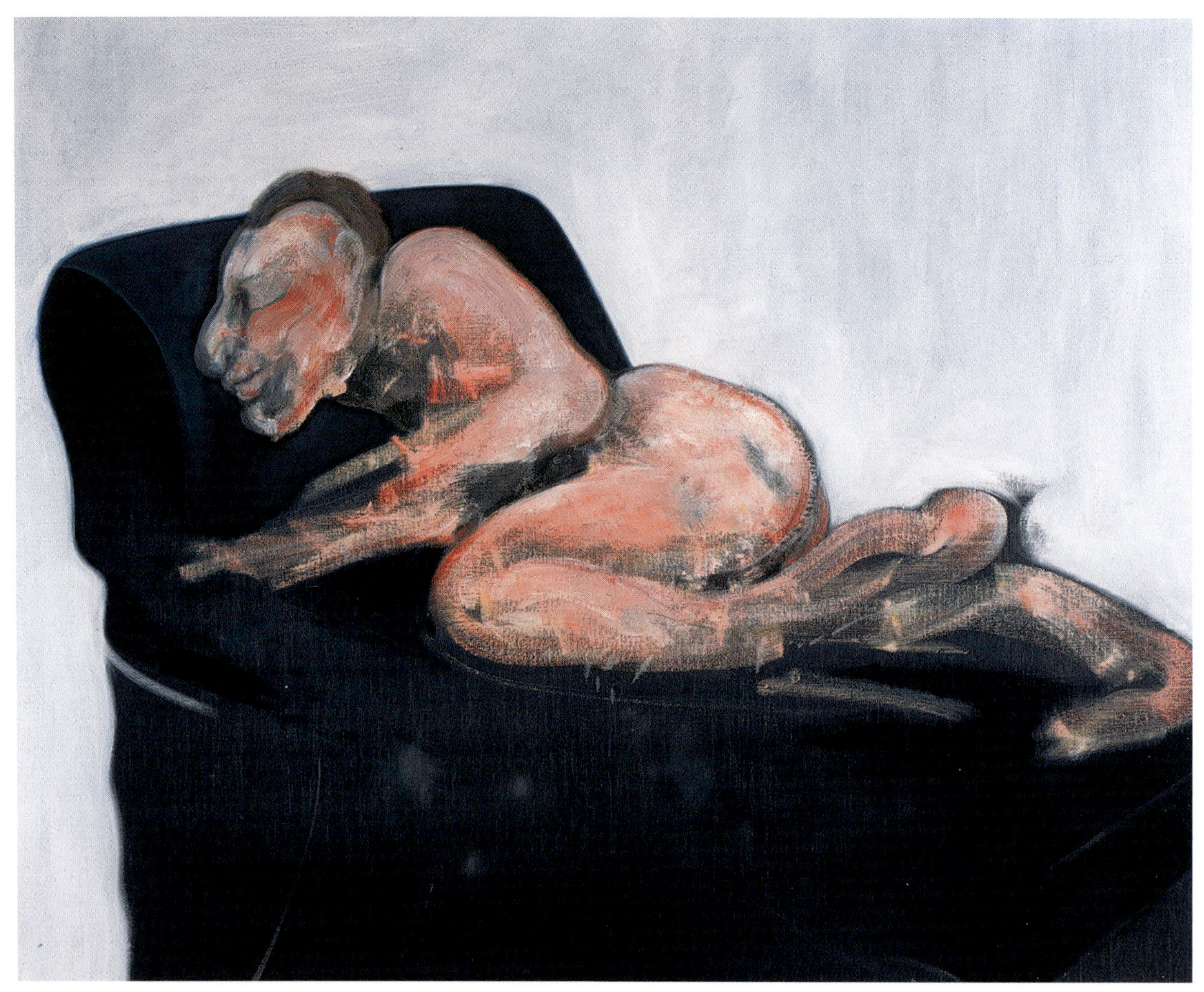

26 | SLEEPING FIGURE, 1959

Oil on canvas · 119.5 × 152.5cm
Private collection

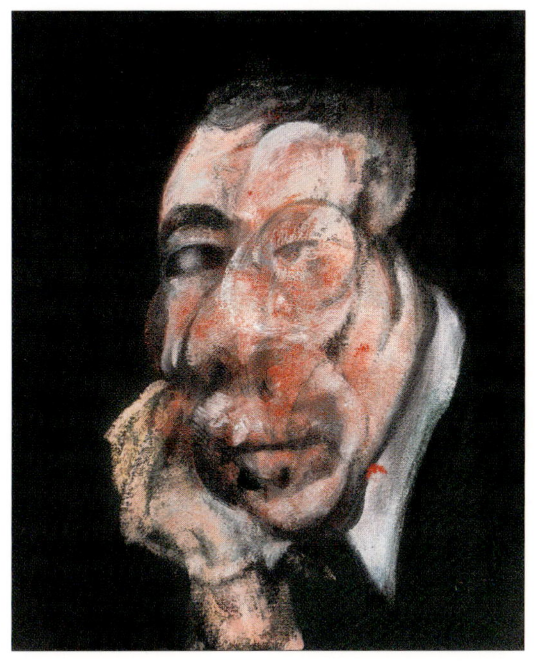

27 | HEAD III, 1961

Oil on canvas · 35.5 × 30.5cm
Private collection

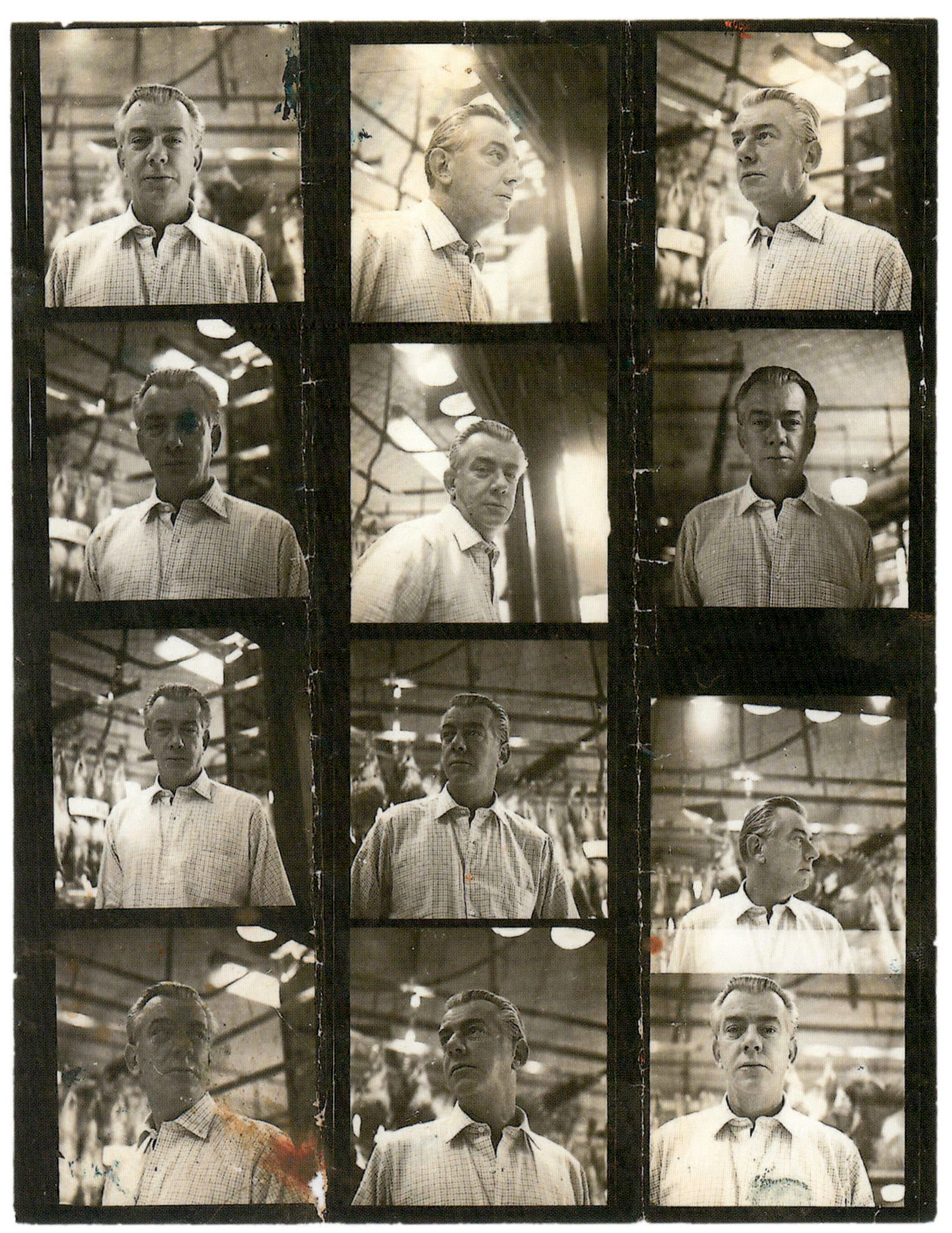

John Deakin *Contact sheet of photographs of Peter Lacy, c.*1959
Dublin City Gallery The Hugh Lane

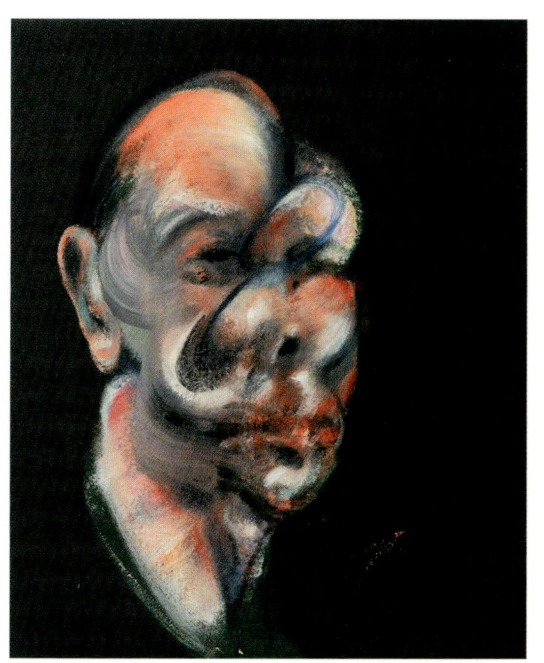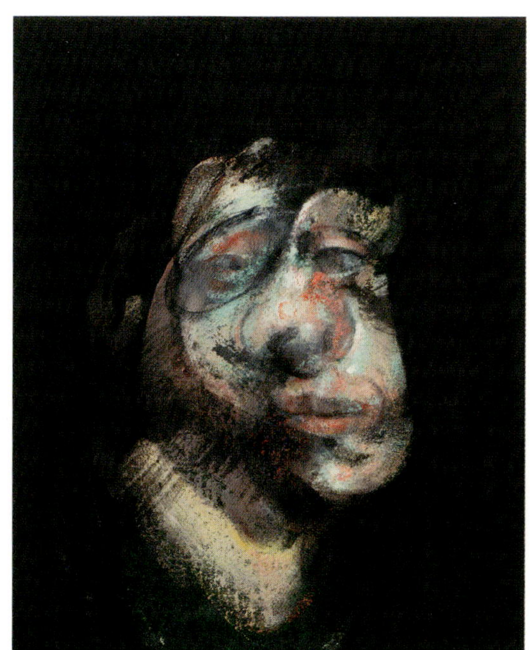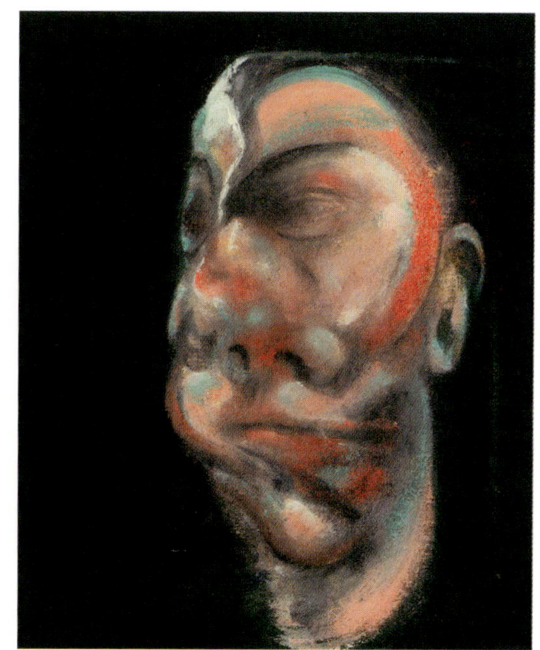

28 | STUDY FOR THREE HEADS, 1962

Oil on canvas (triptych), each 35.5 × 30.5cm
The Museum of Modern Art, New York
The William S. Paley Collection

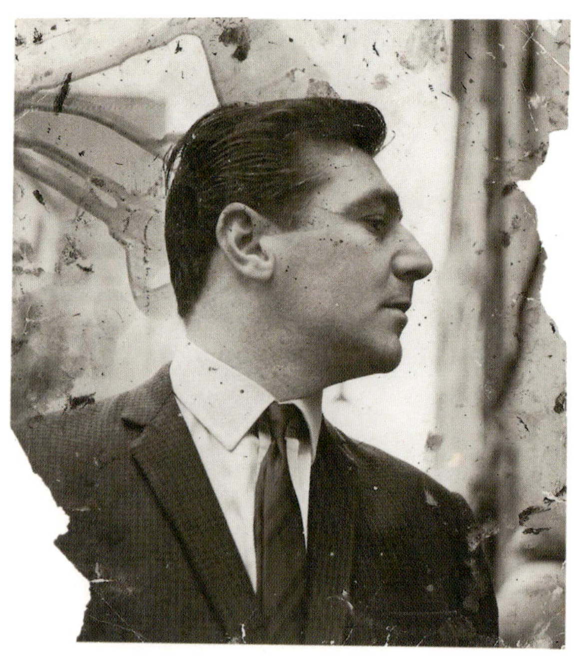

John Deakin *George Dyer, c.*1964
Dublin City Gallery The Hugh Lane

George Dyer (1934–1971) was a young, semi-literate petty criminal whom Bacon met in Soho in 1963. He soon replaced Lacy as Bacon's lover and model – Bacon's first triptych of Dyer (29) was completed the year they met – and was the inspiration for many of his grandest and most moving paintings of the male nude, including a handful of large-scale triptychs commemorating Dyer's death in 1971 from an overdose of sleeping pills exacerbated by alcohol.

In the early 1960s Bacon commissioned the photographer John Deakin to take black and white portrait photographs of some of his favourite subjects – Dyer, Freud, Belcher, Isabel Rawsthorne, Henrietta Moraes – as a substitute for their actual presence in the studio, while he tried to recall their likeness on canvas. In their sharpness and attention to detail, however, Deakin's photographs are in startling contrast to what Bacon actually produced. *Study for Head of George Dyer* (30) shows how Bacon imaginatively transcended his sources. Nothing in Deakin's photograph anticipates the colour and vitality that Bacon injects into the image – the sense of jerking and straining in Dyer's contorted face, one eye closed, muscles tensed, as if trying to get words out of his mouth. (He in fact had a stammer.) The full-length *Portrait of George Dyer in a Mirror* (31), while demonstrating Bacon's interest in reflections and enclosed circular spaces, resembles painted collage – as if one or more of Deakin's photographs had been cut or torn and its fragments pieced together to form a new perceptual synthesis. Bacon also introduces a strong sense of movement in this picture – movement of both the subject and the viewer, as in futurist art.

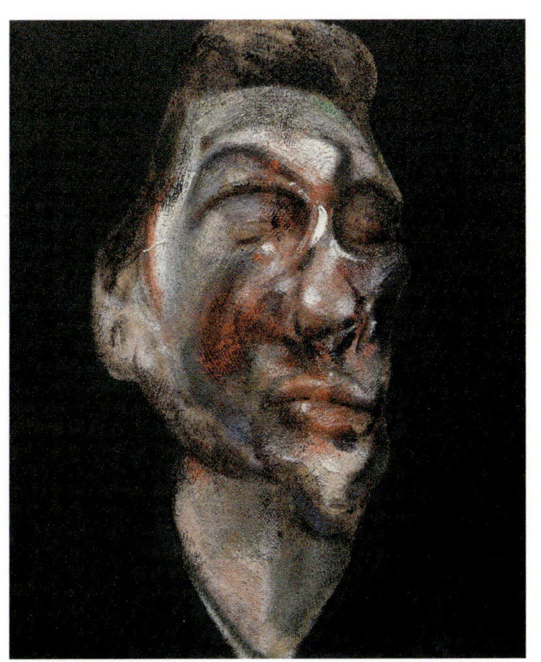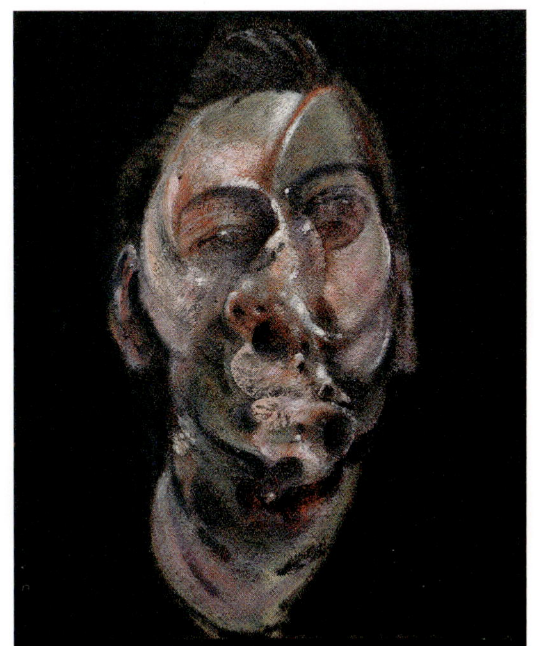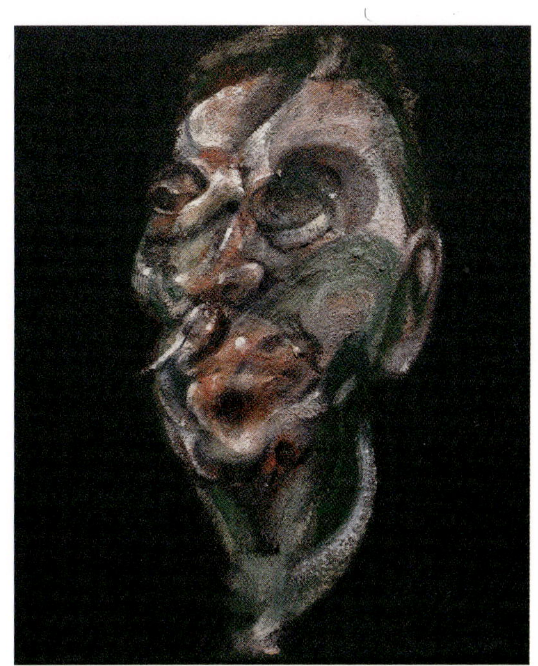

29 | THREE STUDIES FOR A PORTRAIT OF GEORGE DYER, 1963

Oil on canvas (triptych), each 35.5 × 30.5cm
Private collection

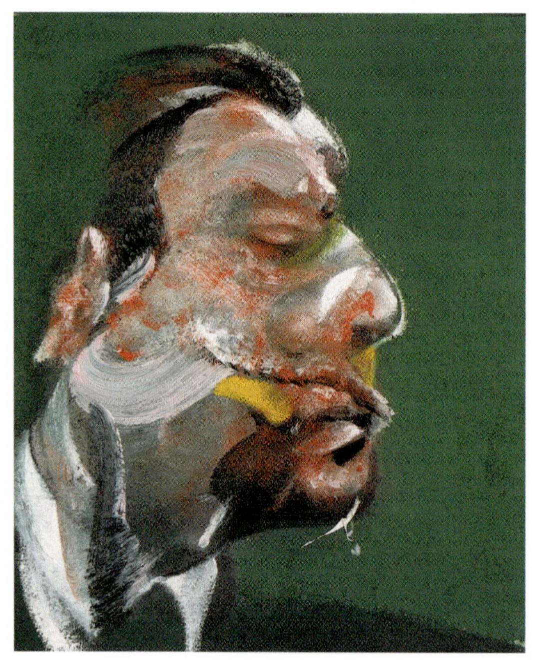

30 | STUDY FOR HEAD OF GEORGE DYER, 1967

Oil on canvas · 35.5 × 30.5cm
Private collection

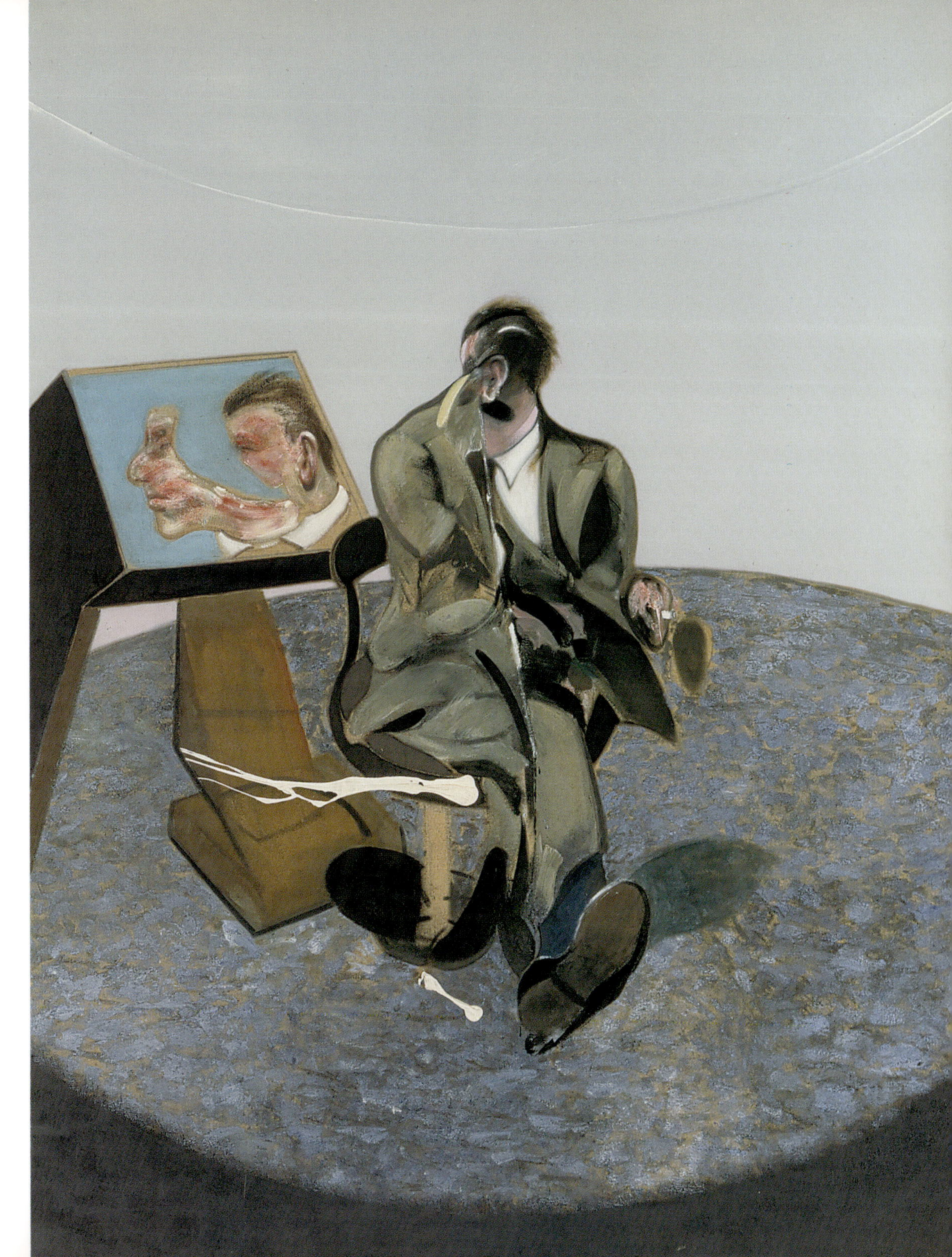

31 | PORTRAIT OF GEORGE DYER

IN A MIRROR, 1968

Oil on canvas · 198 × 147.5cm
Museo Thyssen-Bornemisza, Madrid

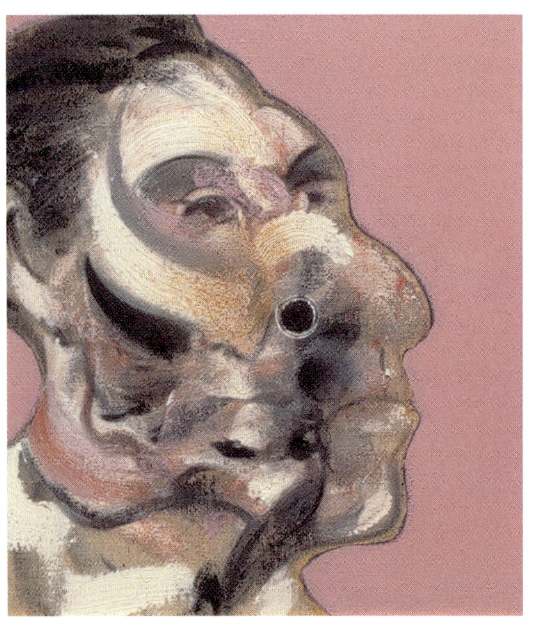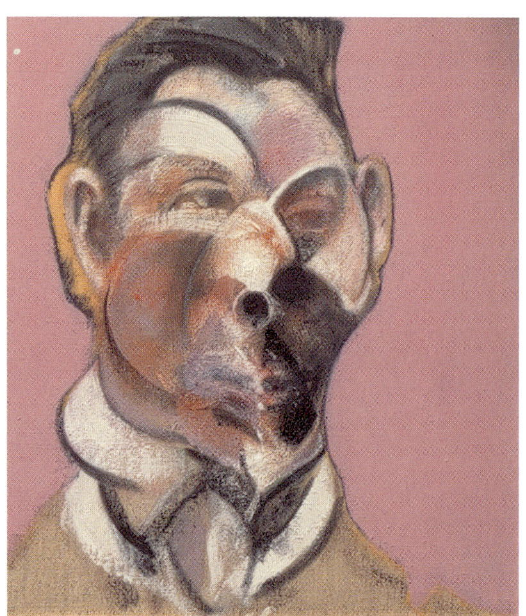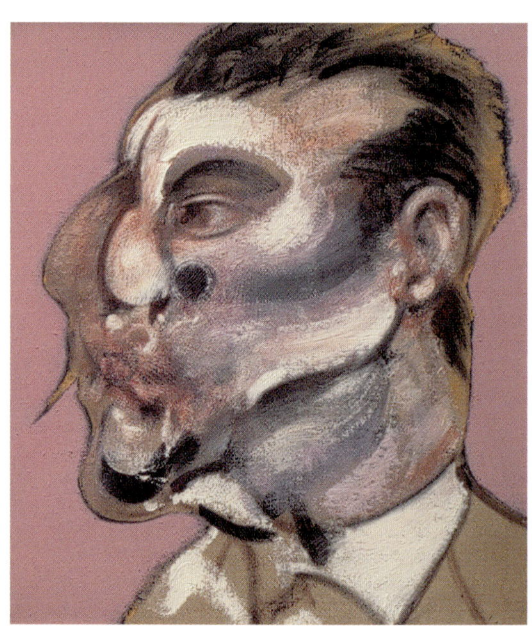

32 | THREE STUDIES OF GEORGE DYER, 1969

Oil on canvas (triptych), each 35.5 × 30.5cm
Louisiana Museum of Modern Art, Humlebaek, Denmark
Donation: The New Carlsberg Foundation

Self-Portraits 1963–87

In 1975 Bacon told David Sylvester: 'I loathe my own face, but I go on painting it only because I haven't got any other people to do.' His first self-portraits date from the 1950s and his own image remained a constant subject in his art from then on.

The first picture in this section (33) is a masterful example of Bacon's mature style: a large, seated full-length in which the formal languages of head and body are in perfect harmony (not always the case with Bacon's figures). No portrait better exemplifies Lawrence Gowing's designation of Bacon as 'a realist … a discoverer of actual presence in paint'. Equally uncompromising is the predominantly green triptych of 1967 (34), with its increasingly radical dismantling of the face from left to right. Although Bacon was essentially a serial painter, such narrative or 'cinematic' development is unusual in his small triptychs. In *Three Studies for Portraits including Self-Portrait* (35), he juxtaposes his own image (right panel) with those of his friends Bruce Bernard (left panel) – the picture editor and historian of photography – and Denis Wirth-Miller (centre). *Self-Portrait* (36) is a touching representation of late-middle age, of coming to terms with one's face but still trying to keep up appearances (the faint suggestion of lipstick and died hair). The performative element in Bacon, a number of whose self-portraits were based on poses adopted in photo booths, sometimes while drunk, cannot be ignored.

In his twenties, Bacon appears to have become a devotee of early avant-garde cinema, especially the films of Buñuel and Eisenstein. In early Soviet – as well as in German Expressionist – cinema, facial close-ups frequently interrupt the main narrative. Whether Bacon was familiar with German Expressionist cinema is not recorded, although it seems likely, given that he lived in Berlin for a few months in 1927. There he was photographed in close-up by Helmar Lerski, who worked as a cameraman on films such as Fritz Lang's *Metropolis*. The cinematic close-up had a powerful influence on the development of portrait photography. Lerski went on to take extreme close-up photographs of anonymous, working-class Berliners which highlighted their universal or archetypal characteristics rather than their individuality.

Bacon said he saw images in sequences and sometimes thought of making a film. Books on portrait photography and physiognomic expression in the 1920s and 1930s often illustrated three different views of the same head side by side in triptych format. Bacon compared his small triptychs to 'police records' in which the suspect is photographed in three contrasting positions – right profile, full-face and three-quarter view (left side).

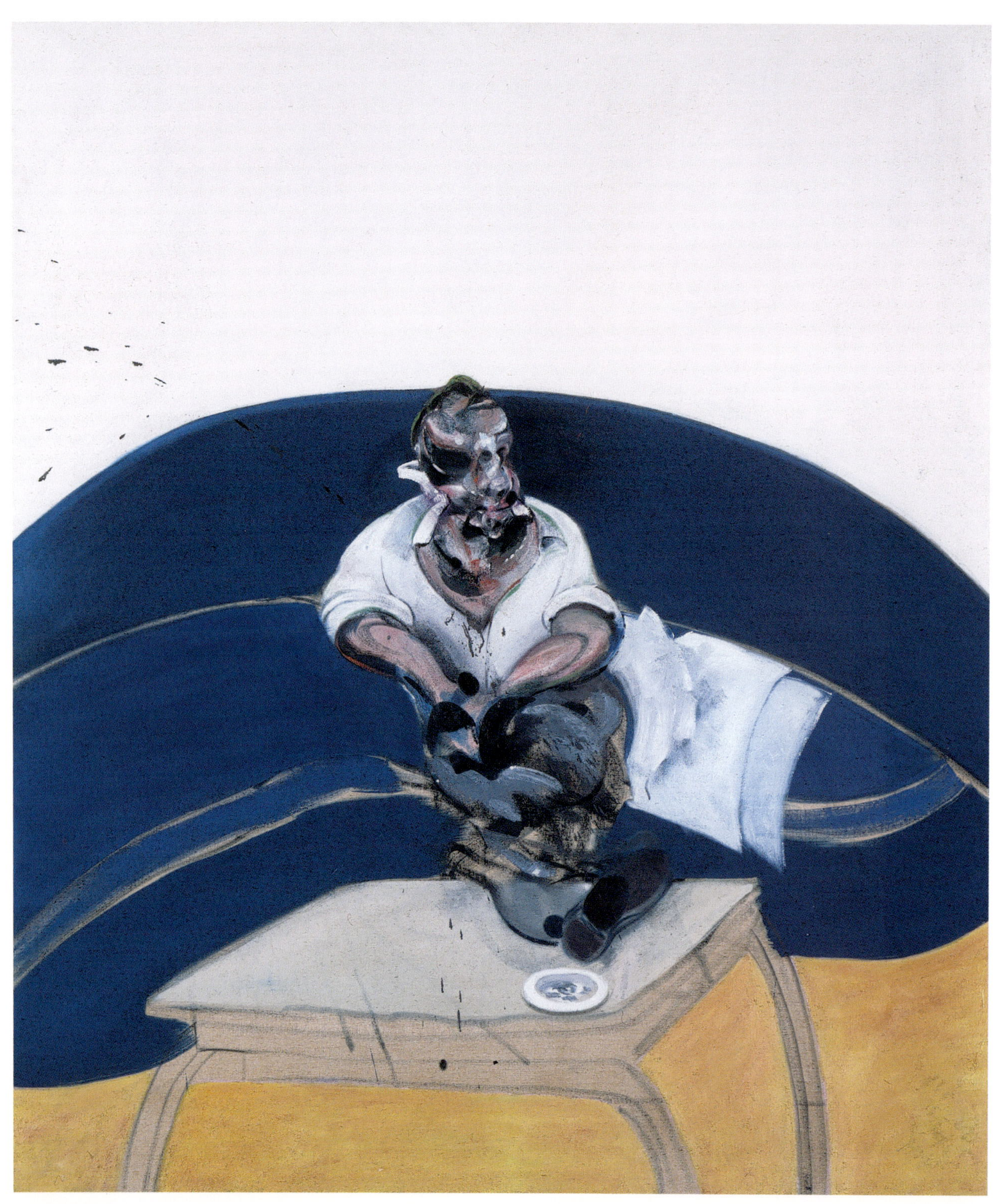

33 | STUDY FOR
SELF-PORTRAIT, 1963
Oil on canvas · 165 × 145cm
National Museums and
Galleries of Wales

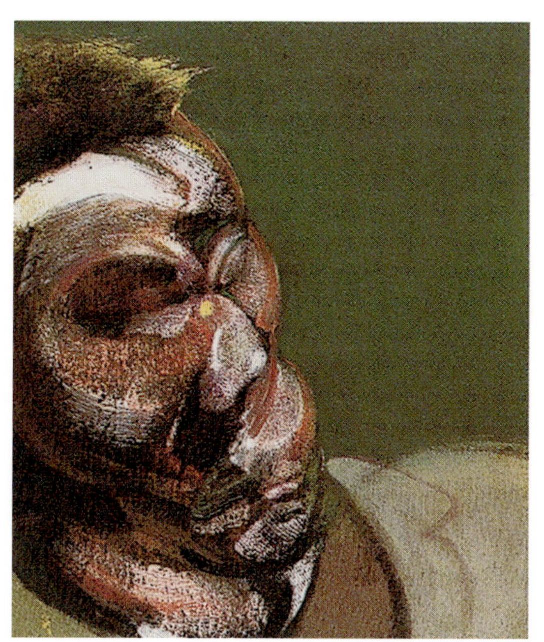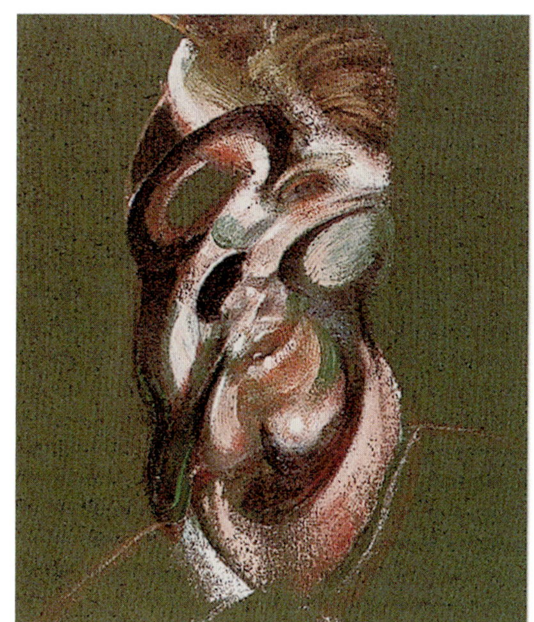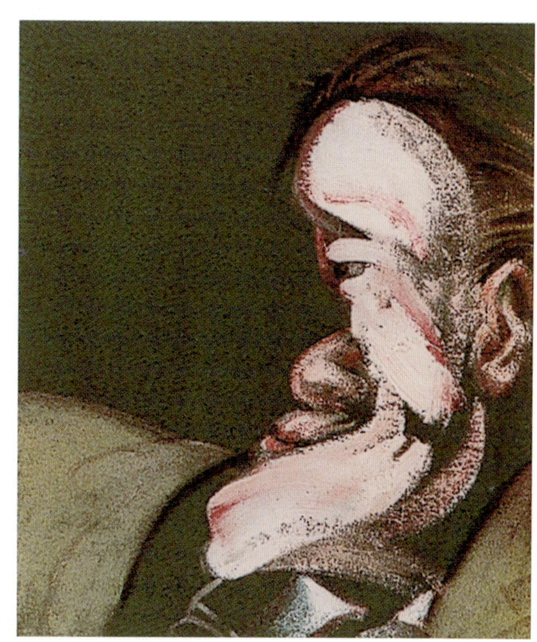

34 | THREE STUDIES FOR A SELF-PORTRAIT, 1967

Oil on canvas (triptych), each 35.5 × 30.5cm
Private collection

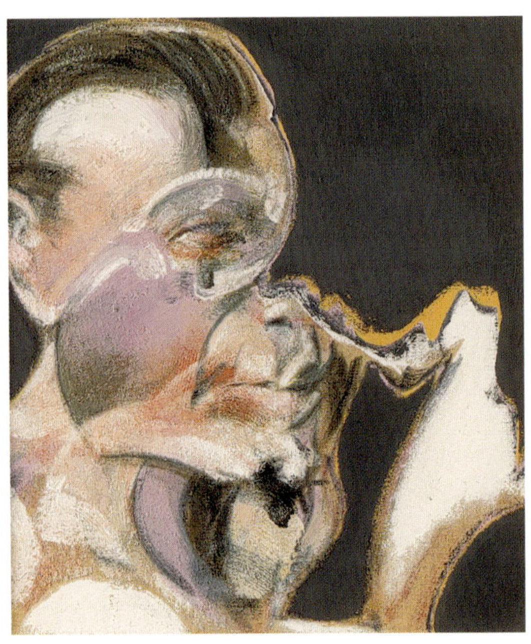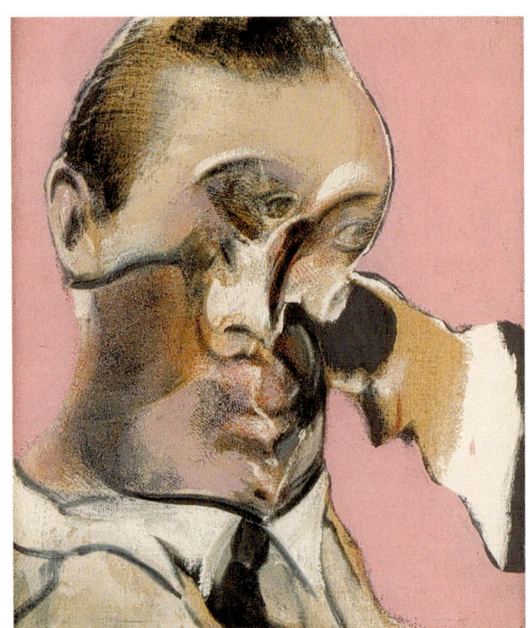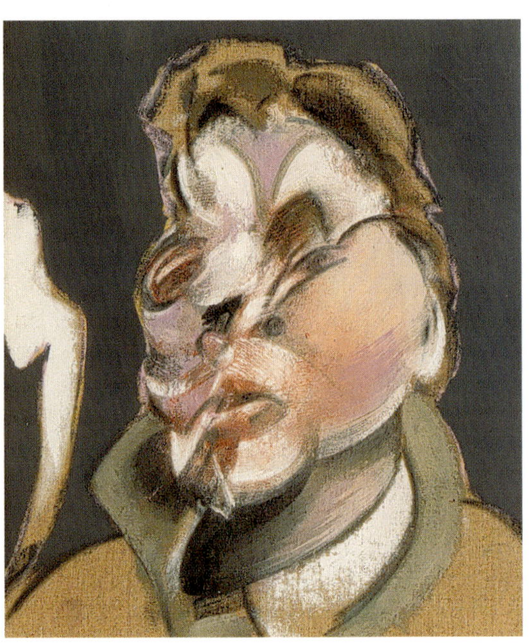

35 | THREE STUDIES FOR PORTRAITS

INCLUDING SELF-PORTRAIT, 1969

Oil on canvas (triptych), each 35.5 × 30.5cm
Private collection

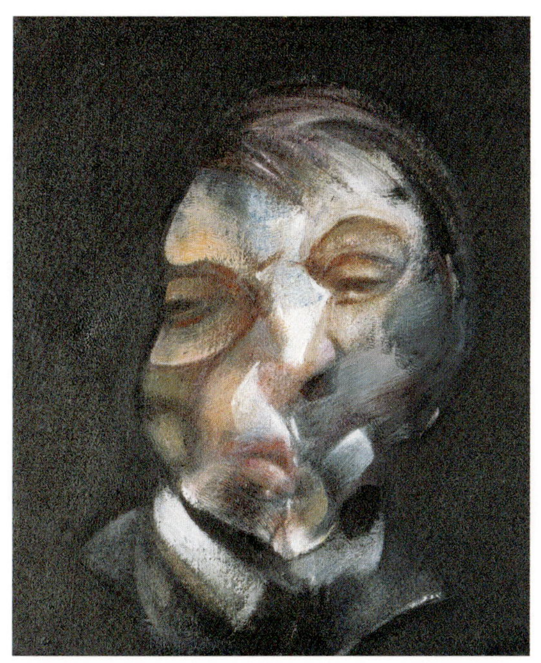

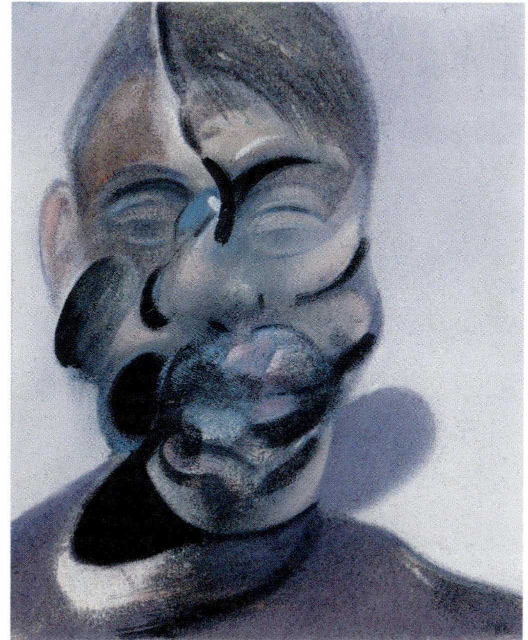

36 | SELF-PORTRAIT, 1971

Oil on canvas · 35.5 × 30.5cm
Musée National d'Art Moderne, Centre Georges Pompidou, Paris
Gift of Louise and Michel Leiris, 1984

37 | SELF-PORTRAIT, 1974

Oil on canvas · 35.5 × 30.5cm
Private collection
Courtesy Timothy Taylor Gallery, London

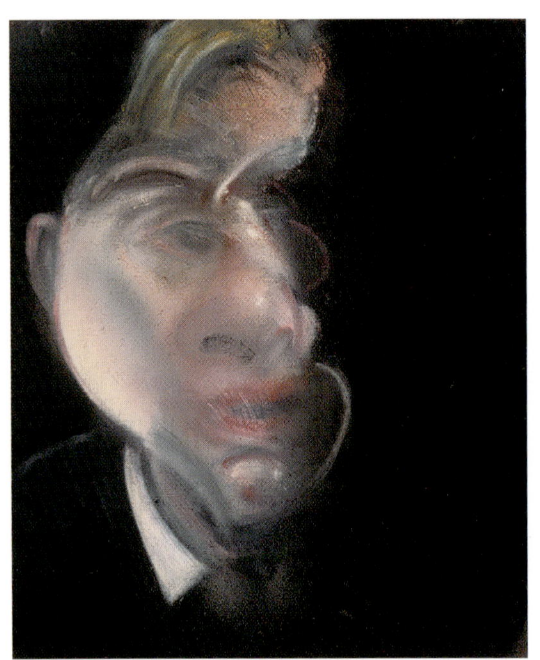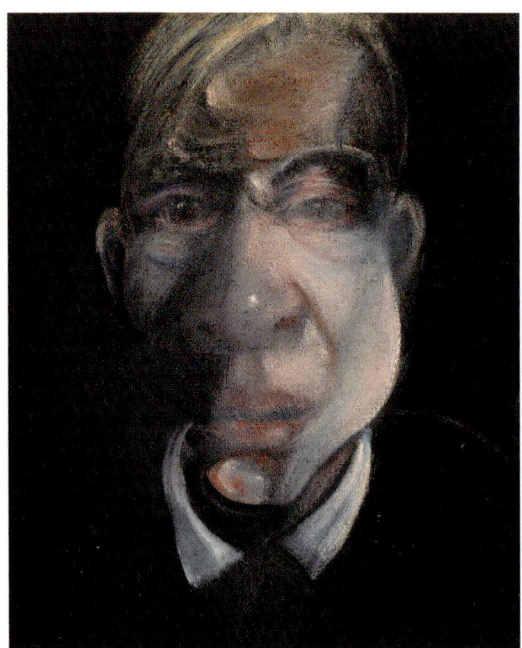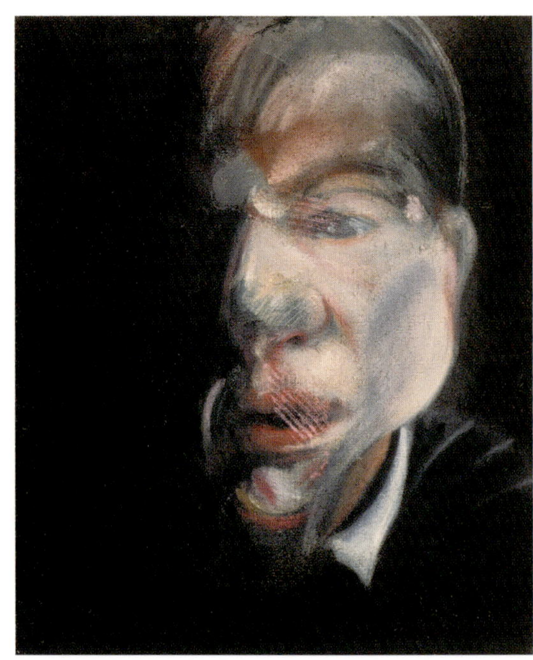

Oil on canvas (triptych), each 35.5 × 30.5cm
The Metropolitan Museum of Art, New York
Jacques and Natasha Gelman Collection, 1998

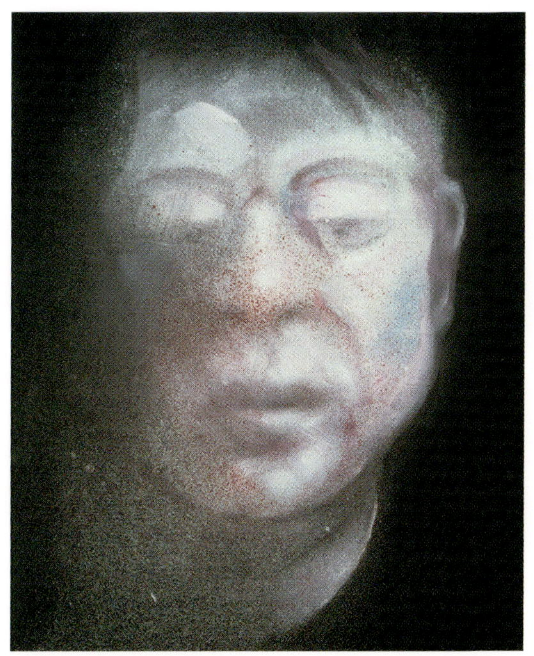

39 | SELF-PORTRAIT, 1987

Oil on canvas · 35.5 × 30.5cm
Private collection
Courtesy Timothy Taylor Gallery, London

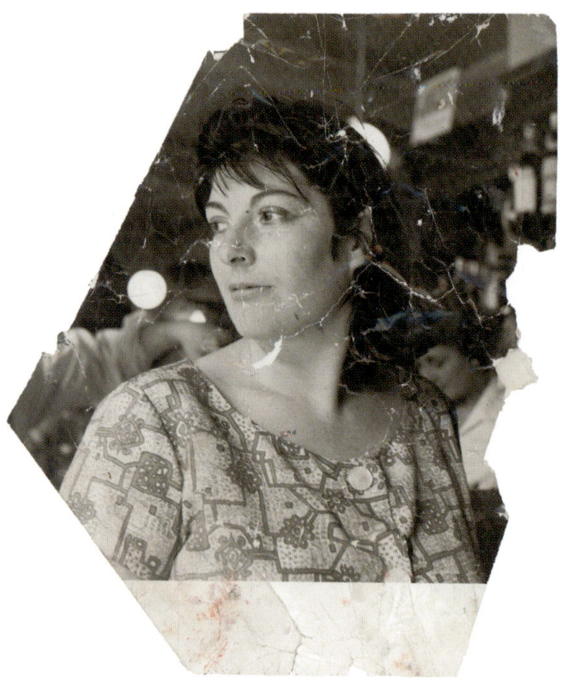

John Deakin *Henrietta Moraes,* 1960s
Dublin City Gallery The Hugh Lane

72

An habitué of Soho in the fifties and sixties, Henrietta Moraes (1931–1999), born Audrey Wendy Abbot, whose third husband was the Indian poet Dom Moraes, was the subject of some of John Deakin's most explicit photographs. Showing her ripe, curvaceous body sprawling on a mattress, they formed the basis of Bacon's most convulsive paintings of the female nude.

In the portraits in this section, also derived from photographs by Deakin, Bacon concentrates on Moraes's head, moving in closer in the two works from 1969 to explore her face. John Russell describes Bacon's method in these and other heads as one of 'superimposition' of different appearances and states in the same image, similar to the techniques of montage and dissolve in film. Bacon's small triptychs, however, cannot be read developmentally from left to right. Each panel is independent and self-contained, displaying an individual characteristic of the subject with an intensity 'not encountered in life'. In *Portrait of Henrietta Moraes* (42), the stark profile of the head, reminiscent of an African tribal mask (filtered, perhaps, through Picasso), is thrown into almost sculptural relief by the expanse of flat yellow background.

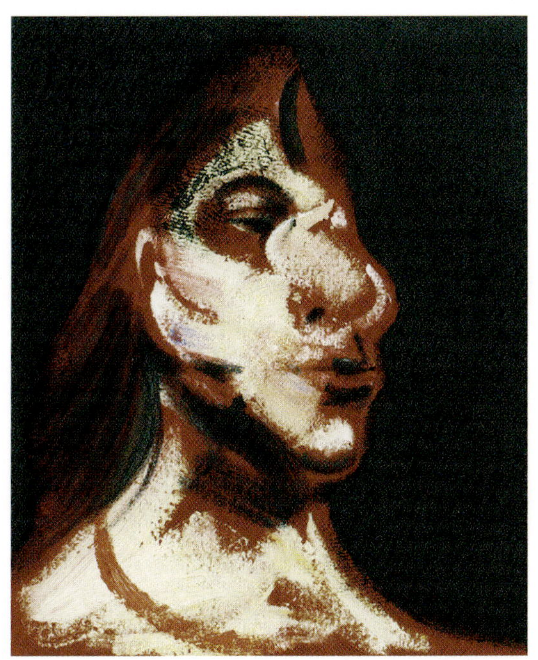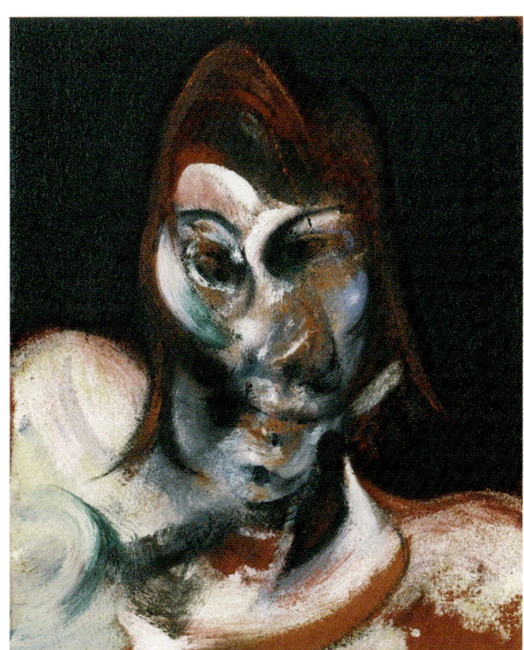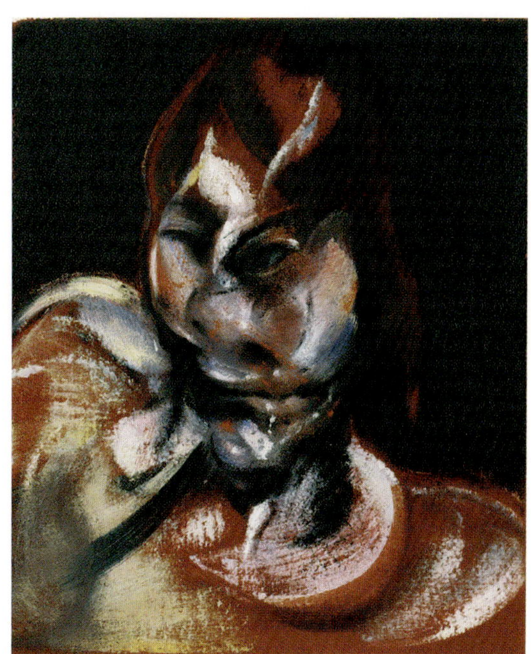

40 | THREE STUDIES FOR PORTRAIT OF HENRIETTA MORAES, 1963

Oil on canvas (triptych), each 35.5 × 30.5cm
The Museum of Modern Art, New York
The William S. Paley Collection

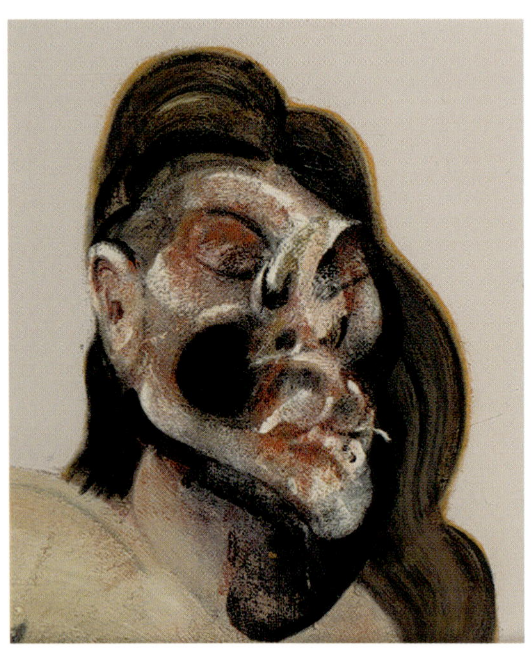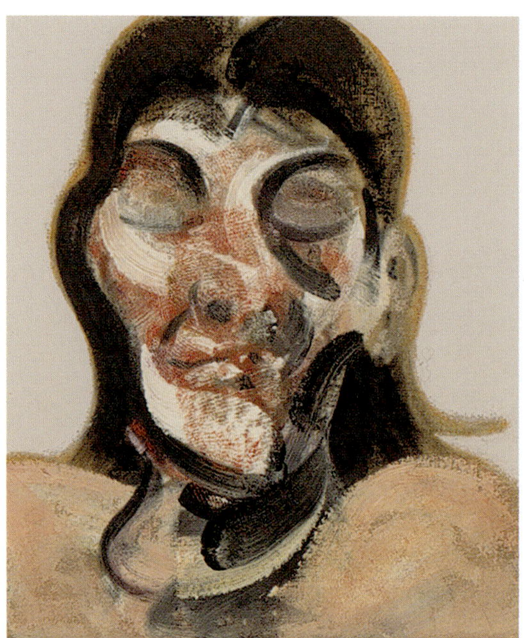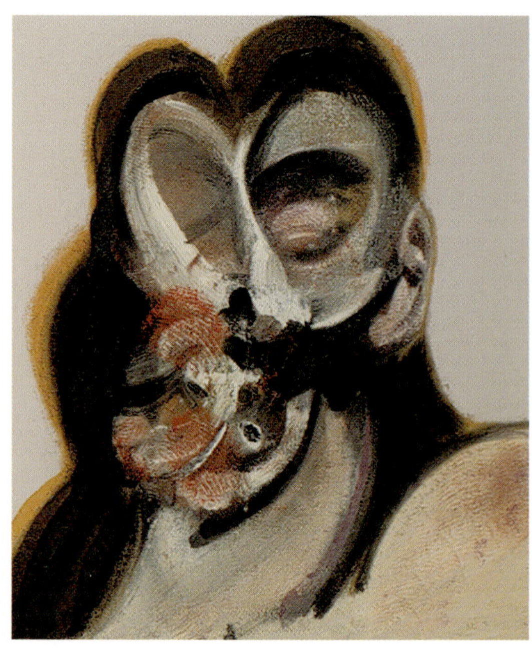

41 | THREE STUDIES FOR PORTRAIT OF HENRIETTA MORAES, 1969

Oil on canvas (triptych), each 35.5 × 30.5cm
Private collection

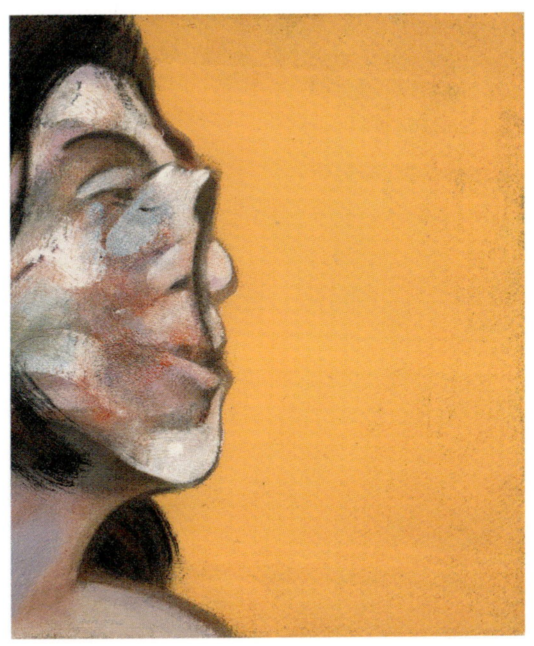

42 | PORTRAIT OF HENRIETTA MORAES, 1969

Oil on canvas · 35.5 × 30.5cm
Private collection

Lucian Freud 1964–67

All five works in this section portray the painter Lucian Freud, either alone or with friends of Bacon's: Isabel Rawsthorne, fellow painter Frank Auerbach, and John Hewett ('J.H.'), a noted dealer in antiquities and ethnographic art.

Freud (b.1922) first heard about Bacon from Graham Sutherland at the end of the Second World War and soon became a close friend, for a while seeing him on a daily basis. Their closeness may be inferred from the fact that in three of the portraits brought together here Bacon seems to have projected onto Freud's image elements of his own body and body language. For example, in the left-hand panel of *Double Portrait of Lucian Freud and Frank Auerbach* (43), Freud's arms, trunk and thighs have much of the soft, round fleshiness that we associate with Bacon's body. Similarly, in the two triptychs included here, Freud is depicted with his left hand stroking or resting on his forehead, a gesture typical of Bacon recorded in photographs and television interviews. In spite of this degree of (probably unconscious) identification with his subject, in all the small portraits in this section Bacon has brilliantly caught the shape and leanness of Freud's face – the contours of cheekbone, jaw and nose – as well as its lithe, mobile quality. In *Three Studies for Portrait of Lucian Freud* (44), Freud's head seems to expand and contract against the blood-red background, like some pulsating organism. *Study for Head of Lucian Freud* (47) is one of Bacon's more extraordinary images of a kind of twisting or pivoting motion: the rapid curved brushstrokes of bright green paint across the forehead and eyes have no rational explanation but feel perfectly natural.

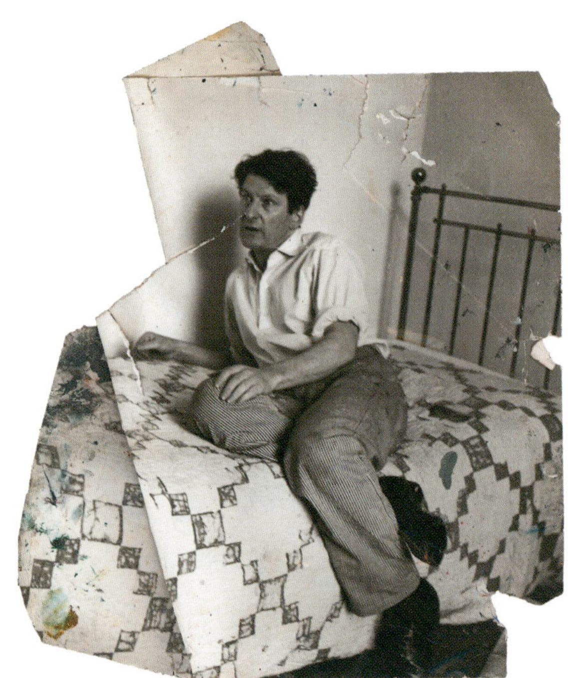

John Deakin *Lucian Freud, c.*1964
Dublin City Gallery The Hugh Lane

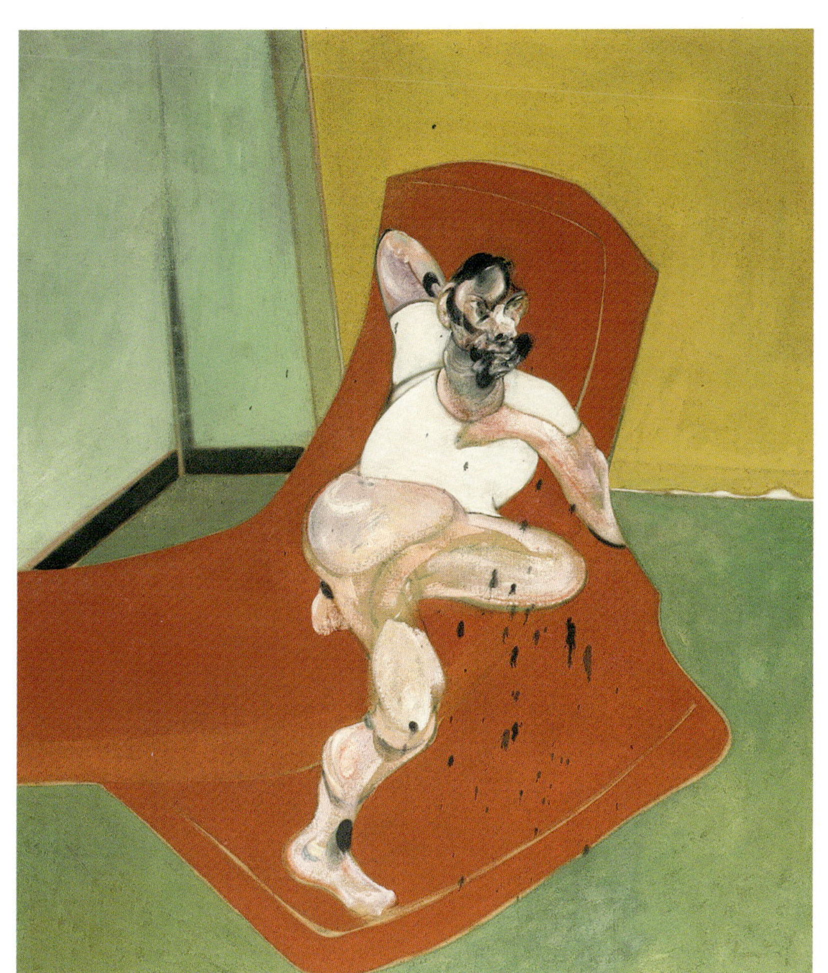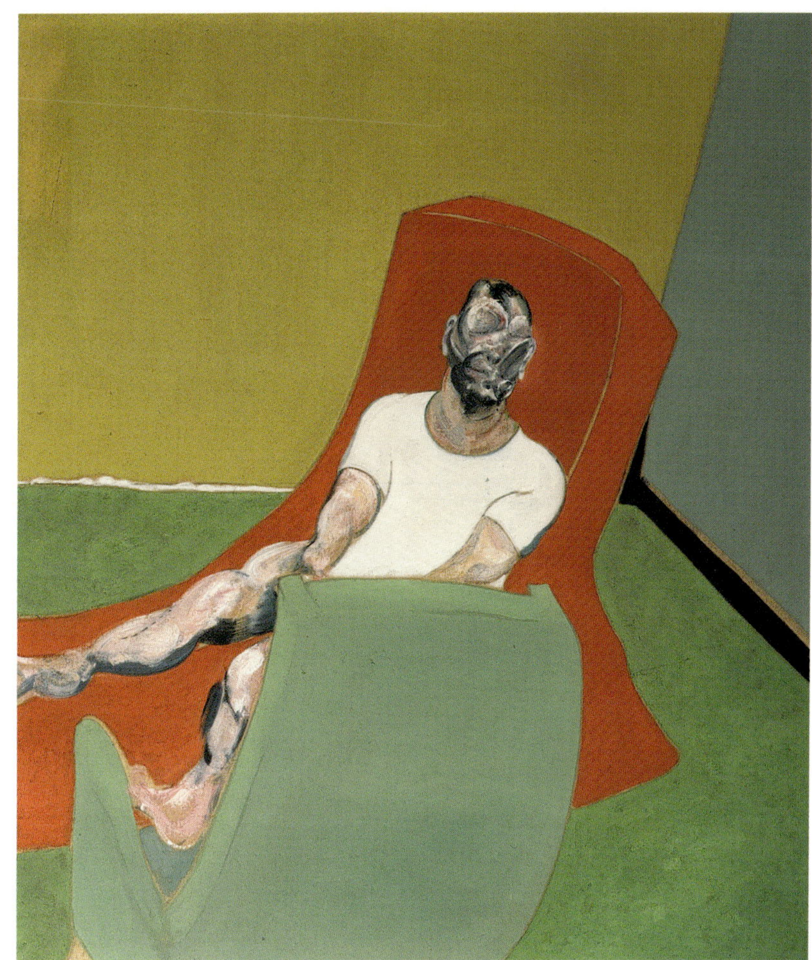

43 | DOUBLE PORTRAIT OF LUCIAN FREUD AND FRANK AUERBACH, 1964

Oil on canvas (diptych), each 165 × 145cm
Moderna Museet, Stockholm

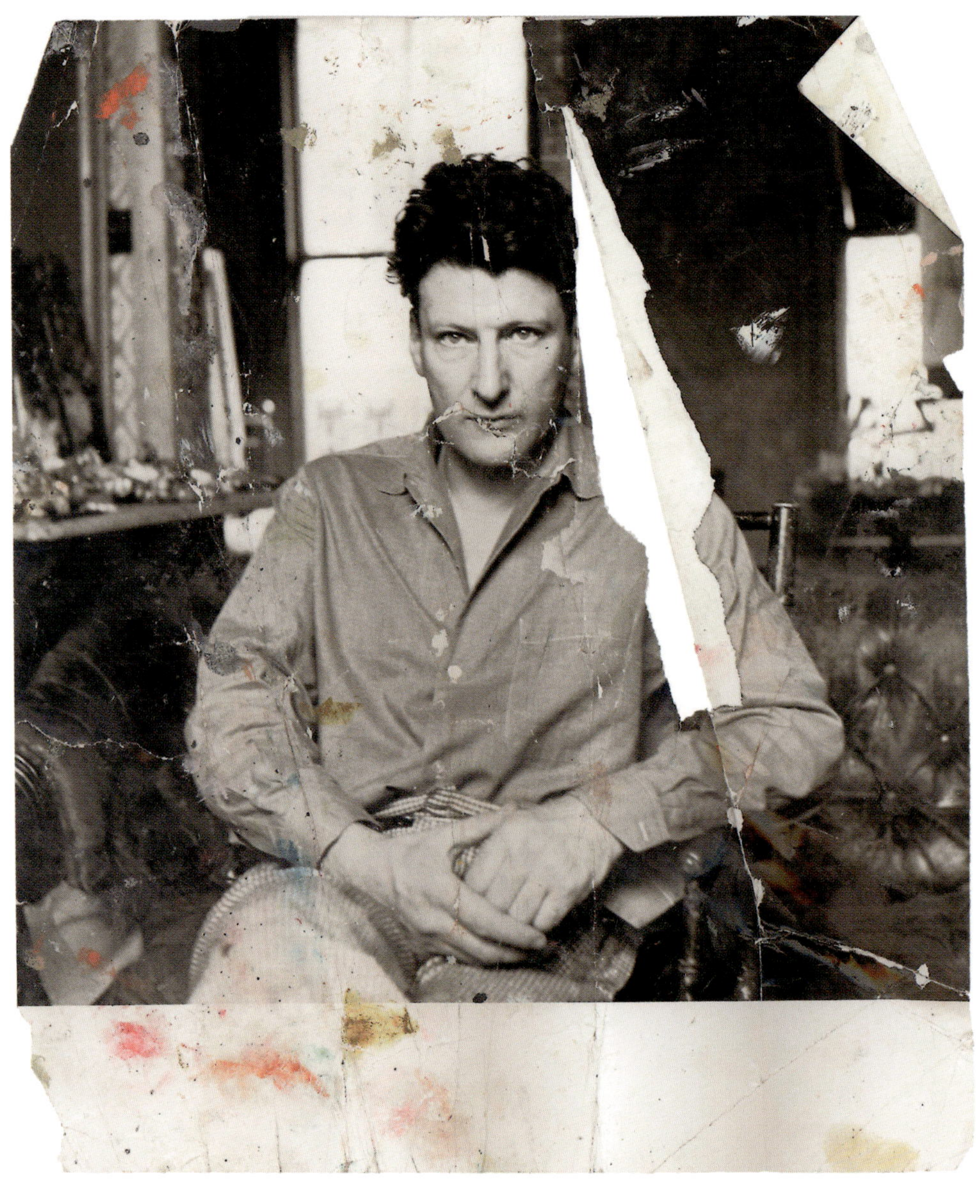

John Deakin *Lucian Freud* 1960s
Dublin City Gallery The Hugh Lane

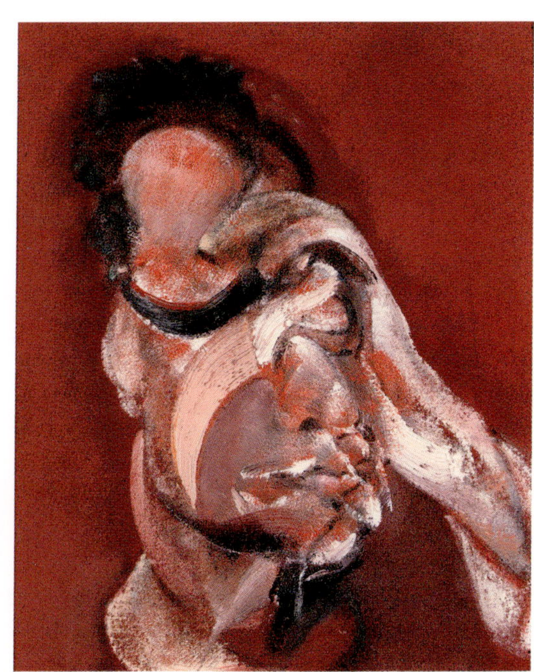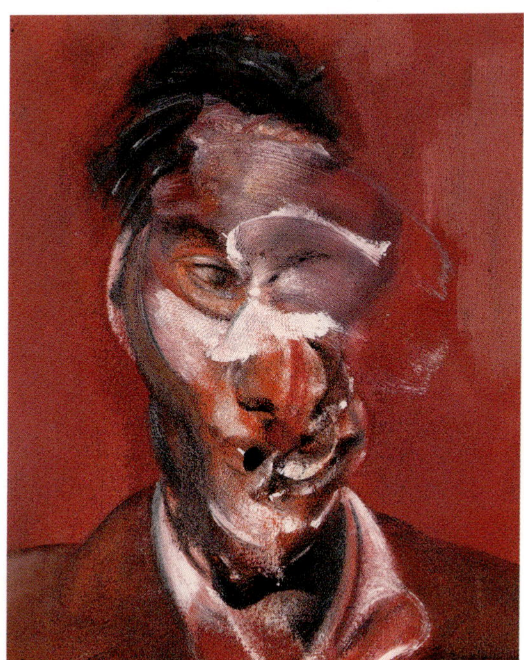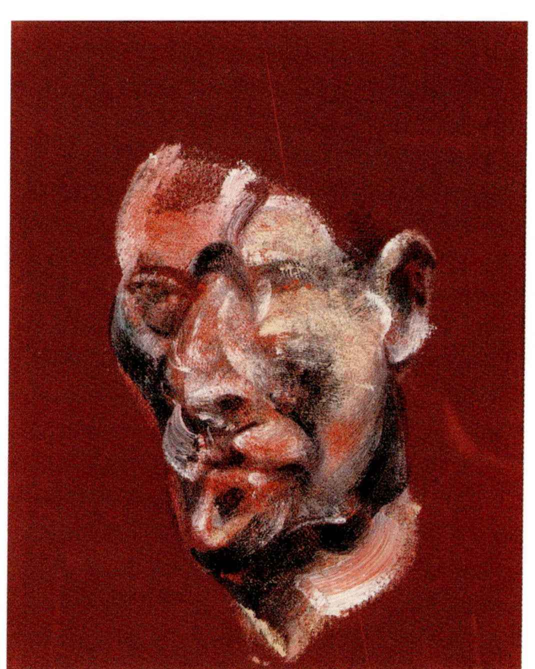

44 | THREE STUDIES FOR PORTRAIT OF LUCIAN FREUD, 1965

Oil on canvas (triptych), each 35.5 × 30.5cm

Yageo Foundation

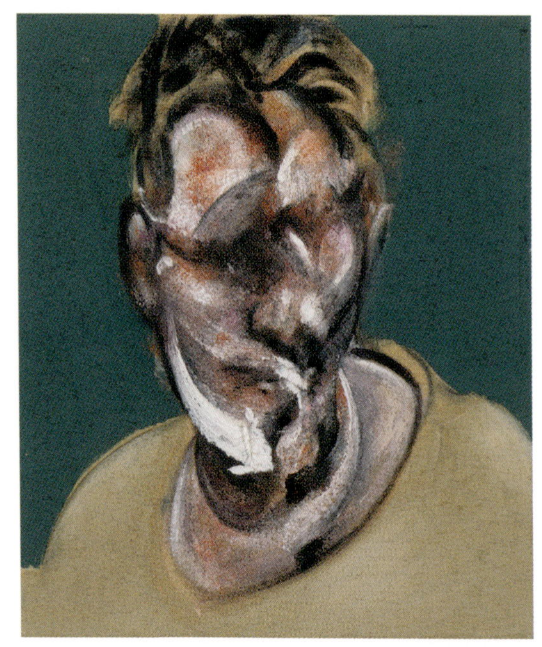

45 | PORTRAIT OF LUCIAN FREUD, 1965

Oil on canvas · 35.5 × 30.5cm
Private collection

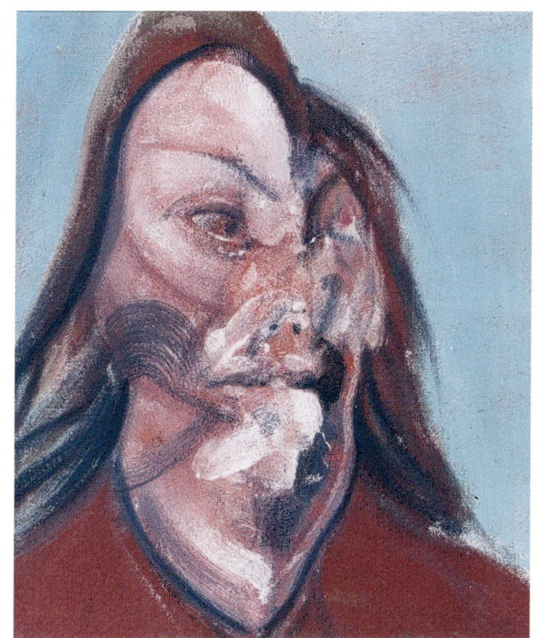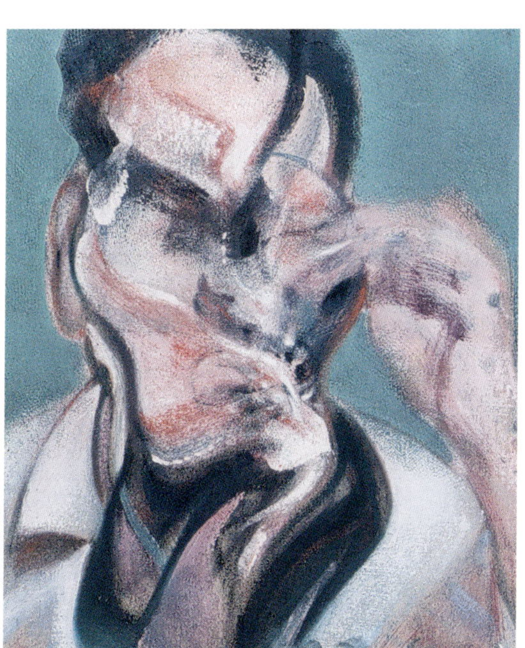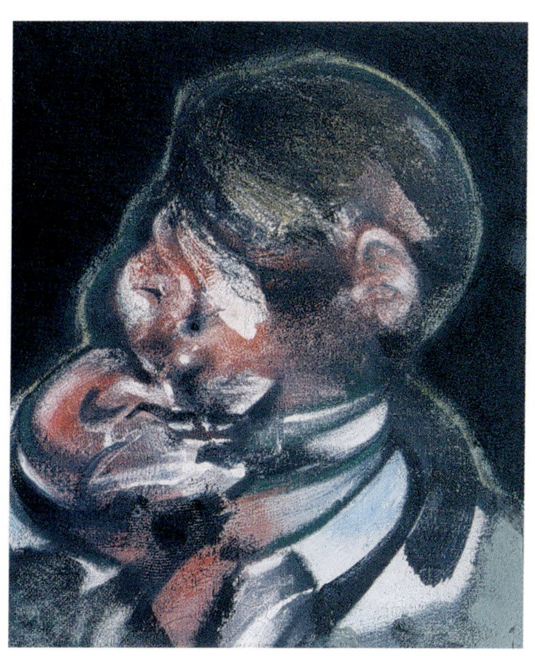

46 | THREE STUDIES FOR PORTRAITS: ISABEL RAWSTHORNE, LUCIAN FREUD AND J.H., 1966

Oil on canvas (triptych), each 35.5 × 30.5cm
Private collection

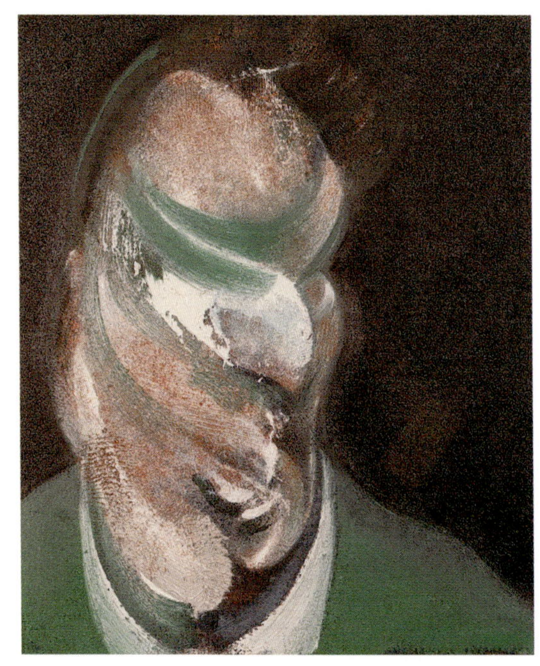

47 | STUDY FOR HEAD OF LUCIAN FREUD, 1967

Oil on canvas · 35.5 × 30.5cm
Private collection

Isabel Rawsthorne 1966–67

Isabel Rawsthorne (1912–1992), born Isabel Nicholas, whose third husband was the composer Alan Rawsthorne, studied painting in London and Paris – where, to finance her studies, she posed for Derain, Giacometti and other artists. She was close to Giacometti, became friends with Michel Leiris, and was for a time the lover of the radical writer Georges Bataille. After the war she married the conductor Constant Lambert and designed ballets for Covent Garden.

Bacon painted more small heads of Rawsthorne than of anyone except himself. As well as examples of these heads, this section brings together three larger portraits, including the famous full-length *Portrait of Isabel Rawsthorne Standing in a Street in Soho* (51). Although based on a Deakin photograph showing Rawsthorne standing outside a glass shopfront, only the background of car and blurred figures (inspired by an image of a bullfight), and the blue awnings flapping behind the subject's head, evoke an exterior location. The circular space and rectangular frame enclosing the figure are more suggestive of an arena or stage. Bacon presents us with a haunting image of isolation and inscrutability, as Rawsthorne appears to turn away from the onlooker lost in thought.

In all five portraits of Rawsthorne, the subject is recognisable from her characteristic high forehead and sweep of hair. Although at times her features seem near to

disintegration, by portraying his subject 'inside out' – for example, bone structure, flesh and blood, as well as eyes, mouth and nose – Bacon captures a strong sense of both her physical presence and her inner dynamism. In *Three Studies of Isabel Rawsthorne* (52), the artist shows not only three different aspects of Rawsthorne's face but paints each one in a different style, ranging from mask-like stylisation to a manner approaching naturalism.

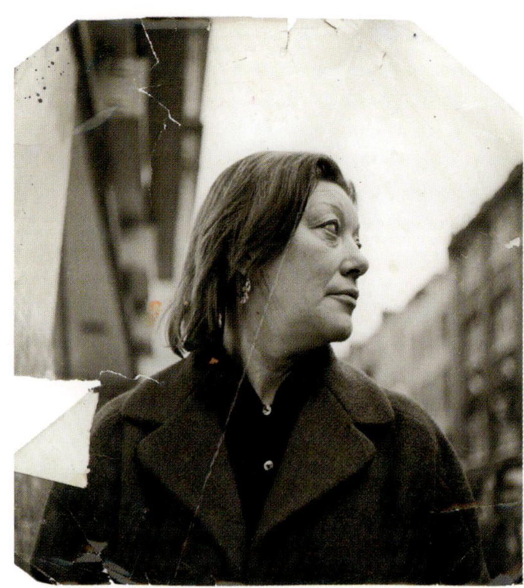

John Deakin *Isabel Rawsthorne, c.*1965
Dublin City Gallery The Hugh Lane

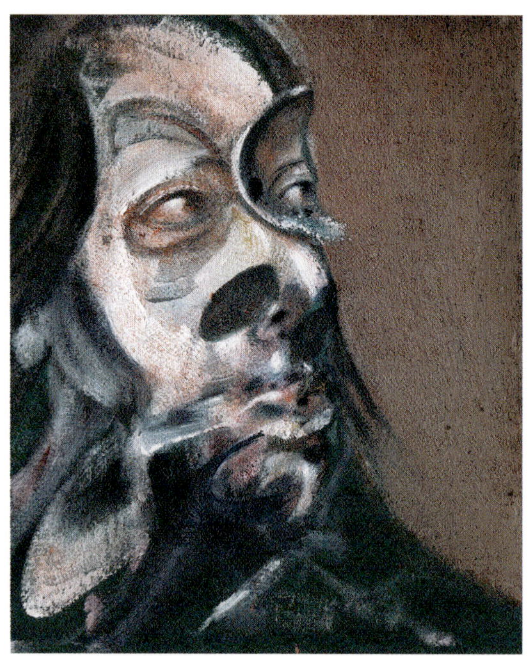

48 | STUDY OF ISABEL RAWSTHORNE, 1966

Oil on canvas · 35.5 × 30.5cm
Musée National d'Art Moderne, Centre Georges Pompidou, Paris
Gift of Louise and Michel Leiris, 1984

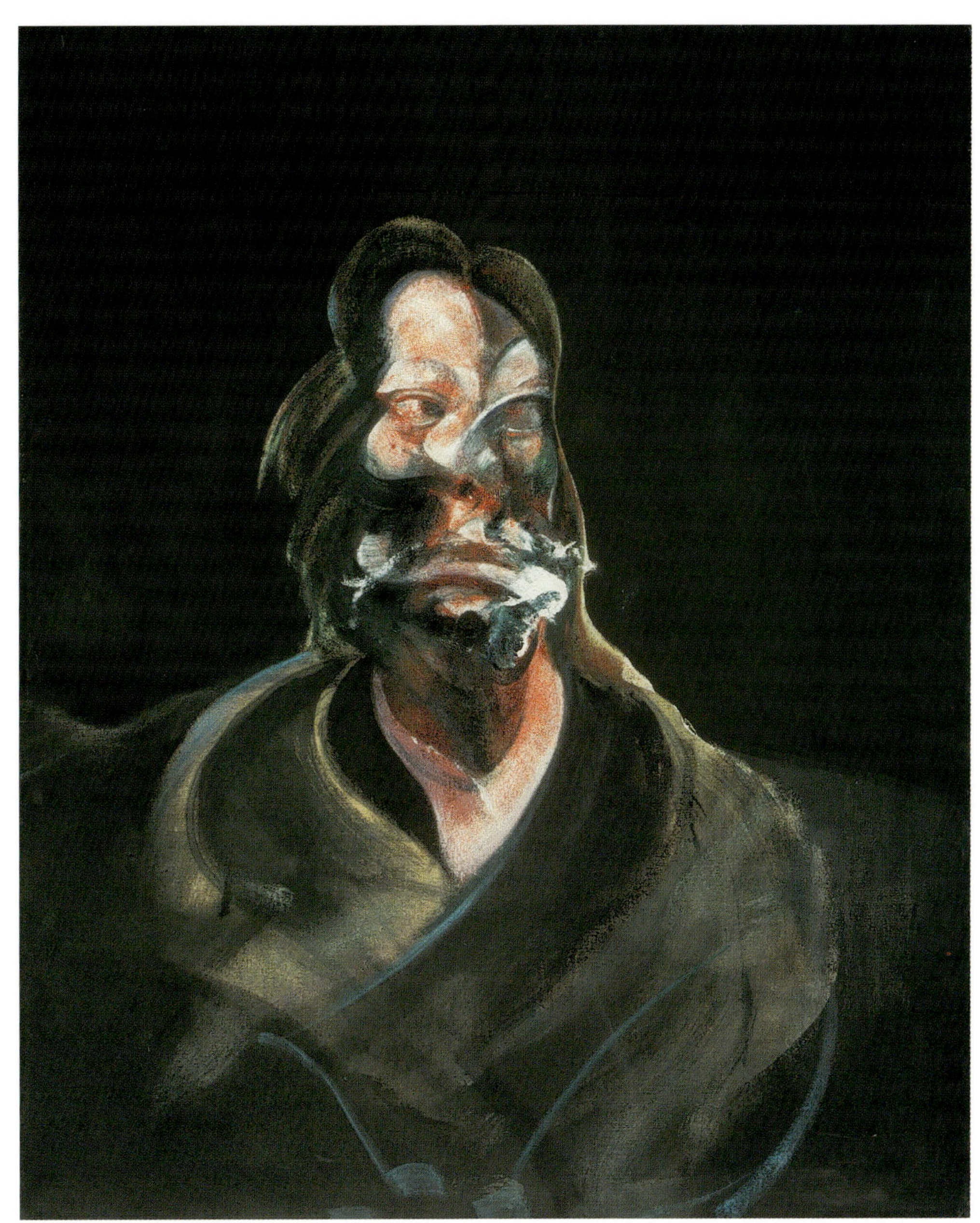

49 | PORTRAIT OF

ISABEL RAWSTHORNE, 1966

Oil on canvas · 81.3 × 68.6cm

Tate. Purchased 1966

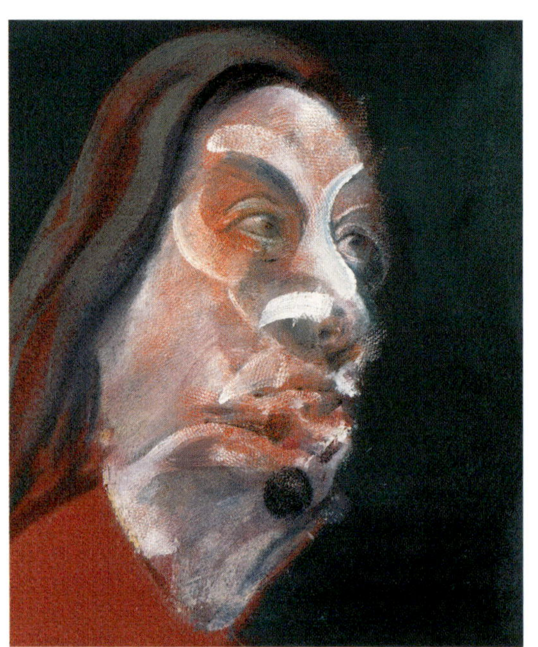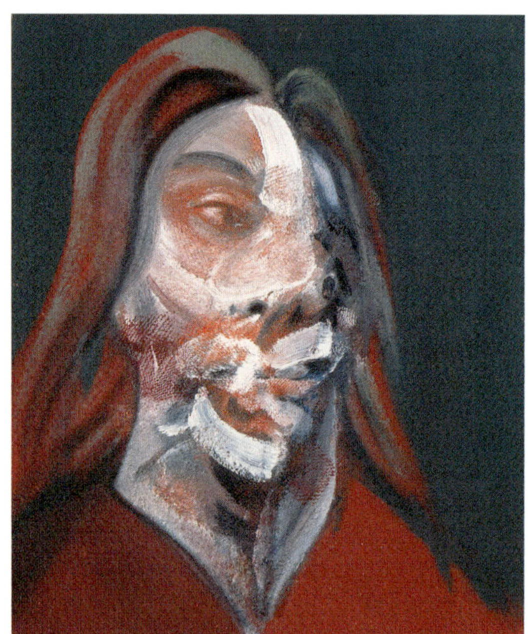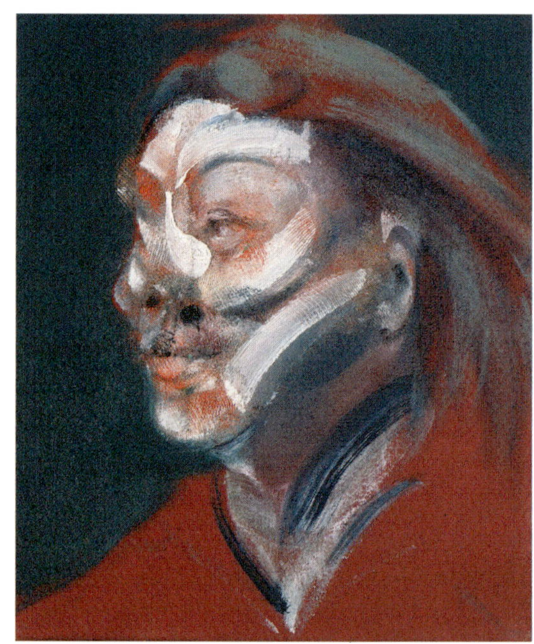

50 | THREE STUDIES OF ISABEL RAWSTHORNE, 1966

Oil on canvas (triptych), each 35.5 × 30.5cm
Private collection

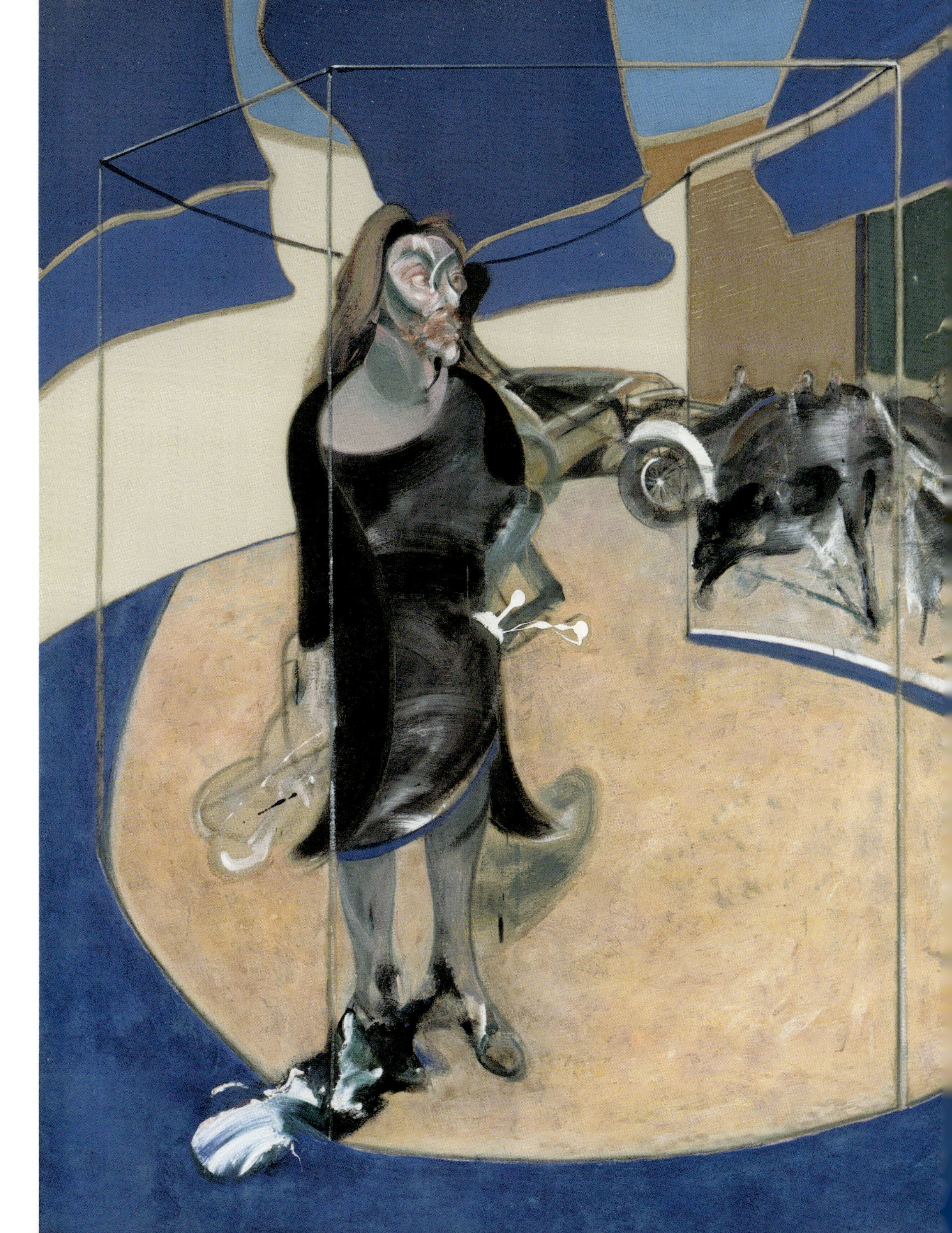

51 | PORTRAIT OF ISABEL
RAWSTHORNE STANDING IN A
STREET IN SOHO, 1967
Oil on canvas · 198 × 147.5cm
Staatliche Museen zu Berlin,
Nationalgalerie

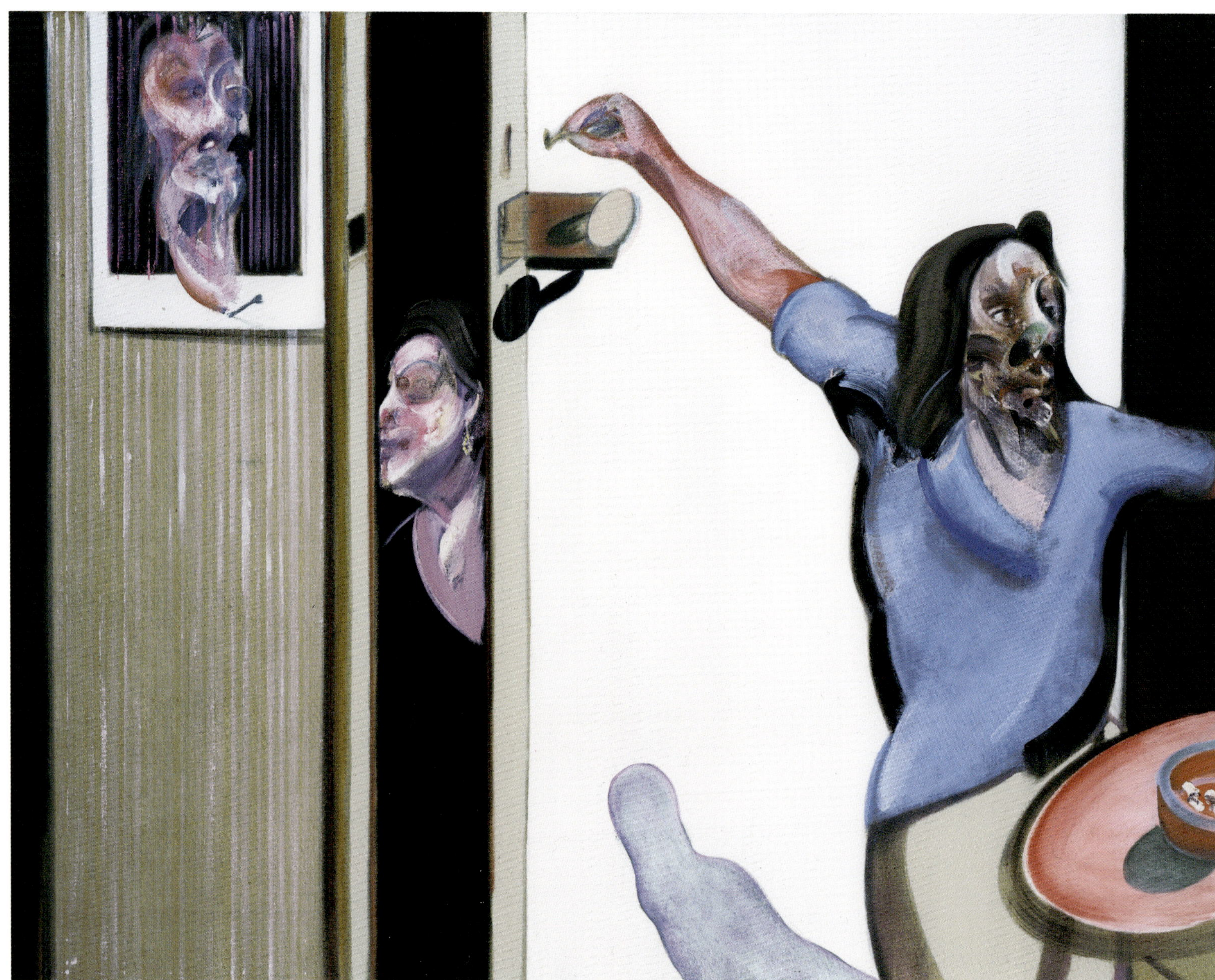

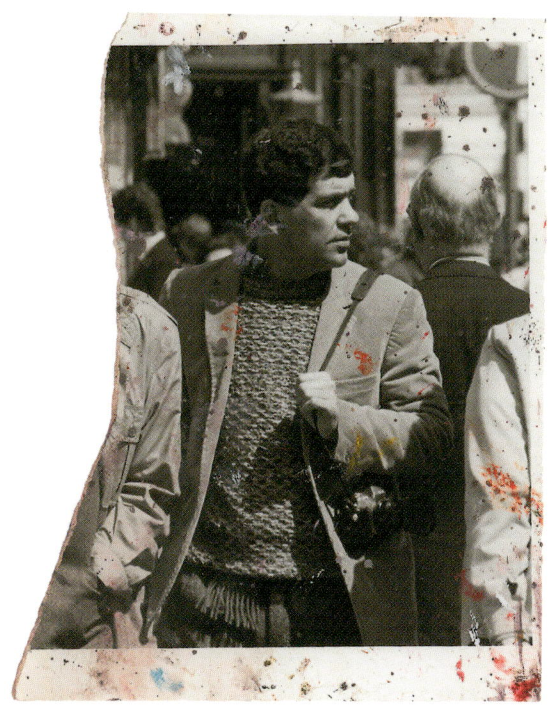

John Edwards, 1985 (still from the *South Bank Show*, LWT)
Dublin City Gallery The Hugh Lane

The two paintings in this last section are moving examples of the more thinly painted and luminous style that characterises Bacon's later work. The subject is shown emerging from a dark background, his bone structure or skull assuming prominence as in an X-ray photograph. Bacon made two portraits of his friend Michel Leiris, the French writer and art critic. Discussing them, he said: 'I'm always hoping to deform people into appearance; I can't paint them literally. For instance, I think that, of those two paintings of Michel Leiris the one I did which is less literally like him [the portrait shown here] is more poignantly like him.'

John Edwards (1950–2003) was an illiterate young East End barman who became Bacon's constant companion from the mid-1970s until the latter's death in 1992. He was the sole beneficiary of Bacon's will and in 1998 donated the artist's studio and its contents to the city of Dublin, Bacon's birthplace.

52 | THREE STUDIES OF ISABEL RAWSTHORNE, 1967

Oil on canvas · 119.5 × 152.5cm
Staatliche Museen zu Berlin, Nationalgalerie

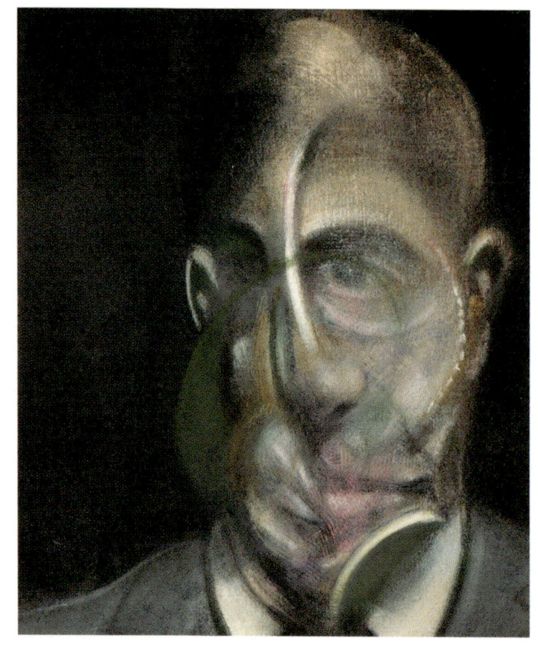

53 | PORTRAIT OF MICHEL LEIRIS, 1976

Oil on canvas · 35.5 × 30.5cm

Musée National d'Art Moderne, Centre Georges Pompidou, Paris

Gift of Louise and Michel Leiris, 1984

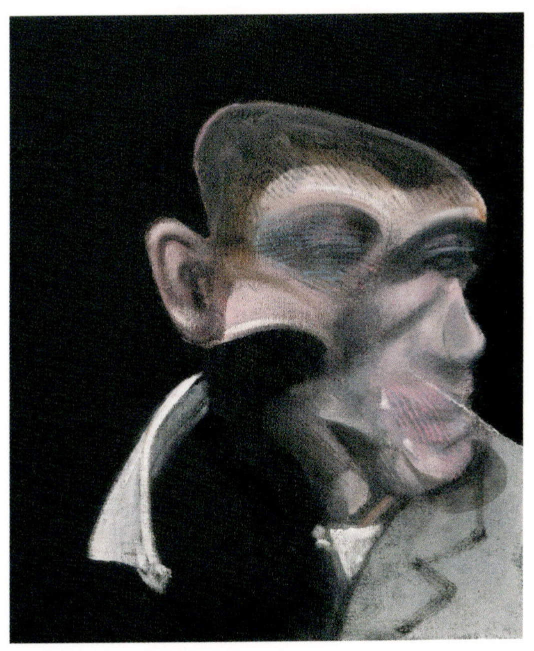

54 | STUDY FOR PORTRAIT OF JOHN EDWARDS, 1989

Oil on canvas · 35.5 × 30.5cm
Private collection, London

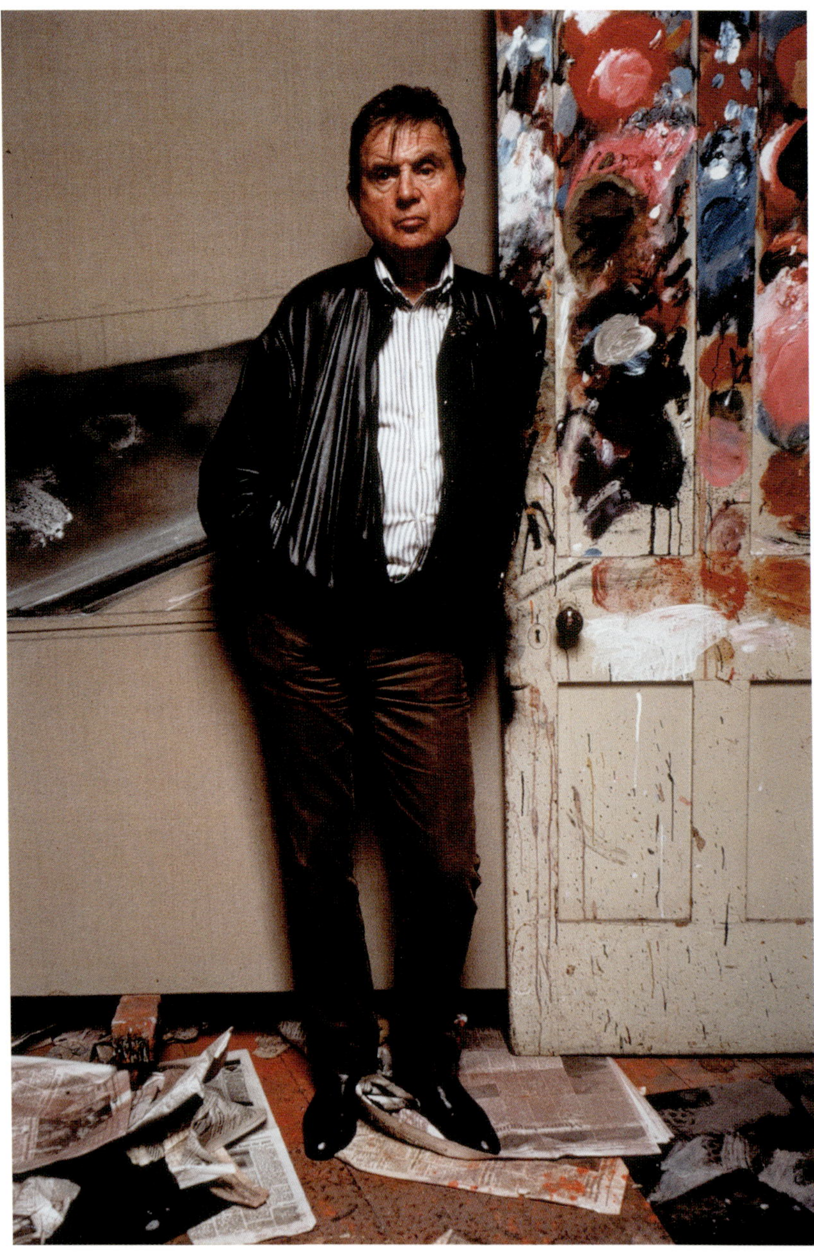

Bruce Bernard *Francis Bacon in his studio*, 1984
Scottish National Gallery of Modern Art

Chronology

1909

Born in Dublin, 28 October, Francis Bacon is the second of five children of English parents, Edward Anthony Mortimer Bacon and Christina Winifred Firth. He has no conventional schooling due to his asthma.

1914–18

During the First World War the Bacon family move to London. Bacon's father works in the War Office.

1924–6

Attends Dean Close School, a boarding school in Cheltenham.

1926

Leaves his family's home in County Kildare, after a row with his father. Lives in London for several months.

1927–8

Spends several months in Berlin and then in Paris. During this period also lives with a French family in Chantilly where he sees Poussin's painting *The Massacre of the Innocents*. Begins to draw and paint after seeing a large exhibition of Picasso's drawings at the Galerie Paul Rosenberg in the summer of 1927. Sees Sergei Eisenstein's film *Battleship Potemkin* and Abel Gance's *Napoleon*.

1929

Following his return to London, moves to 17 Queensberry Mews West, South Kensington. Designs modernist furniture and rugs, and begins to produce his first oil paintings. Holds first exhibition of his work in his studio. Meets Eric Hall, and starts a relationship with him that lasts over fifteen years.

1930

The Studio magazine publishes Bacon's furniture designs under the title 'The 1930 Look in British Decoration'. Arranges a joint exhibition in his studio with the Australian artist Roy de Maistre and the portraitist Jean Shepeard.

1932–3

Moves to Fulham Road, gradually giving up design work in favour of painting.

1933

Moves to 71 Royal Hospital Road, Chelsea. Work included in the reopening exhibition of the Mayor Gallery, Cork Street. Paints a number of crucifixions, the first of which is illustrated in Herbert Read's *Art Now*, opposite Picasso's *Bather*, 1929.

1934

Holds his first solo exhibition at the Transition Gallery, Sunderland House, Curzon Street.

1936

Moves to 1 Glebe Place, Chelsea. His work is rejected by the organisers of the *International Surrealist Exhibition*.

1937

Takes part in the exhibition *Young British Painters*, organised by Eric Hall at Agnew's, London (this includes, among others, De Maistre, Victor Pasmore and Graham Sutherland, who becomes a close friend). His father dies on 1 June.

1939–44

Unfit for active service. Volunteers for Civil Defence and works in the ARP (Air Raid Precautions) until asthma forces his resignation in 1942. Moves to a cottage near Petersfield, Hampshire, which he shares with Eric Hall. Late in 1943 moves to 7 Cromwell Place, South Kensington, formerly the home of artist John Everett Millais. Completes his first major paintings, including the triptych *Three Studies for Figures at the Base of a Crucifixion*, 1944, which is shown at the Lefevre Gallery in 1945 and is subsequently given by Eric Hall to the Tate Gallery, London.

1945–8

Exhibits in several mixed exhibitions at the Lefevre and Redfern Galleries. Erica Brausen, future director of the Hanover Gallery, buys *Painting*, 1946, which is sold in 1948 to The Museum of Modern Art, New York. Stays regularly in Monte Carlo.

1949

Exhibition at the Hanover Gallery, including his series of six *Heads*, 1948–9 (2, 3 & 4) and *Study for Portrait*, 1949 (7). Bacon begins to frequent the drinking clubs, bars and restaurants of Soho, in particular the Colony Room, run by Muriel Belcher. Comes to know, among others, the photographer John Deakin, the writer and photographer Daniel Farson, and artists Timothy Behrens, Lucian Freud, Robert Colquhoun, Robert MacBryde and John Minton, and later, Frank Auerbach and Michael Andrews.

1950

Second exhibition at the Hanover Gallery. Teaches briefly at the Royal College of Art, where he begins to use a studio. Visits mother and sisters in South Africa. Stays briefly in Cairo where he is impressed by ancient Egyptian art.

1951

Gives up 7 Cromwell Place and for the next few years moves frequently. In the Colony Room meets Peter Lacy, a former fighter and test pilot, and begins a long and intense relationship with him. Paints first portrait of Lucian Freud (8) and exhibits a series of three *Popes* (inspired by Velázquez's portrait of Innocent X) at the Hanover Gallery.

1953

First exhibition abroad at Durlacher Brothers in New York. For short time shares a house with the critic David Sylvester, who sits for Bacon.

1954

Exhibition, with Ben Nicholson and Lucian Freud, in the British Pavilion at the Venice Biennale. Paints the *Man in Blue* series (11, 12, 13 & 14).

1955

Moves to Battersea where he stays until 1961. First retrospective exhibition at the Institute of Contemporary Arts, London. Paints series of portraits based on the Life Mask of William Blake (15). Paints commissioned portrait of Robert Sainsbury. Begins series of eight portraits from life of Sainsbury's wife, Lisa, his first female portrait.

1956

Paints first self-portrait and the first of six pictures inspired by Van Gogh. Included in *Masters of British Painting 1800–1950*, The Museum of Modern Art, New York. Visits Peter Lacy in Tangier.

1957

First exhibition in Paris, at the Galerie Rive Droite, with catalogue introduction by Roland Penrose and David Sylvester. Spends summer in Tangier with Lacy.

1958

Leaves the Hanover Gallery and signs contract with Marlborough Fine Art, who remain Bacon's dealers for the rest of his life.

1959

Exhibits in *Documenta II*, Kassel, the Sau Paulo *Biennale* and *New Images of Man*, The Museum of Modern Art, New York. Eric Hall dies.

1960

First exhibition at Marlborough Fine Art. The photographer Cecil Beaton sits for his portrait; Bacon destroys the work shortly after.

1961

Moves to 7 Reece Mews, South Kensington, which remains his home and studio until his death.

1962

Paints first large triptych, *Three Studies for a Crucifixion*. First major retrospective held at the Tate Gallery, London. Learns on the eve of the opening of Peter Lacy's death in Tangier. Paints first small triptych, *Study for Three Heads* (28), showing his own self-portrait flanked by heads of Lacy. Records conversation with David Sylvester for the BBC, the first of a series of nine, all eventually published.

1963

Retrospective at the Solomon R. Guggenheim Museum, New York. Increasingly paints portraits of identifiable individuals, most of whom are close friends, in particular Muriel Belcher (18), Isabel Rawsthorne (46, 48–52), Henrietta Moraes (40–2) and Lucian Freud (43–7). Begins close relationship with George Dyer, a petty thief whom he meets in a Soho bar, and who becomes his most frequent subject (29–32). Many of these portraits are based on specially commissioned photographs by John Deakin.

1964

Included in *Documenta III*, Kassel. Publication of catalogue raisonné by Ronald Alley and John Rothenstein.

1965

Retrospective at Hamburg Kunstverein. Meets the French writer and philosopher Michel Leiris at the opening of the Alberto Giacometti retrospective at the Tate Gallery.

1966

Exhibition at the Galerie Maeght, Paris, with catalogue introduction by Michel Leiris, whom he later paints (53). Around this time meets the American wildlife photographer and author Peter Beard, whom he also paints.

1967

Awarded the Rubens Prize.

1968

Visits USA for his first exhibition at the Marlborough Gallery, New York.

1971

Major retrospective at the Grand Palais, Paris. Shortly before the exhibition opening, George Dyer dies in Paris as a result of an overdose.

1972–4

Paints series of three large triptychs influenced by the death of George Dyer. Meets John Edwards, who becomes his close friend and, following John Deakin's death, assumes role of photographer for Bacon. Output of self-portraits increases.

1975

Major exhibition at The Metropolitan Museum of Art, New York. Publication of David Sylvester's first four interviews with Bacon. Spends more and more time in Paris.

1977

Highly successful show of new paintings at Galerie Claude Bernard, Paris.

Sources

1978–84
Important exhibitions held in Madrid, Barcelona, London, Tokyo and Paris.

1985
Second retrospective at the Tate Gallery, London, which tours to Stuttgart and Berlin.

1988
Retrospective at the Central House of Art (New Tretyakov Gallery), Moscow.

1989–90
Retrospective at the Hirshhorn Museum and Sculpture Garden, Washington, DC.

1990
Travels to Madrid to see the Velázquez exhibition at the Prado.

1992
On 28 April dies from a heart attack (following pneumonia brought on by his asthma) in Madrid, while visiting a young friend, José Capello. John Edwards named as his sole heir. In 1998 studio and contents are given by John Edwards to the Hugh Lane Gallery, Dublin.

John Russell, *Francis Bacon*, London, 1971 (third edition, 1993)

David Sylvester, *Interviews with Francis Bacon*, London, 1975 (fourth edition, 1993)

Andrew Forge and Lawrence Gowing, *Eight Figurative Painters*, Yale Center for British Art, New Haven, 1981

Dawn Ades and Andrew Forge (with a note on technique by Andrew Durham), *Francis Bacon*, Tate Gallery, London, 1985

Lawrence Gowing and Sam Hunter (with a foreword by James Demetrion), *Francis Bacon*, Hirshhorn Museum and Sculpture Garden, Smithsonian Institution, Washington DC, 1989

William Feaver and John Russell, *Francis Bacon 1909–1992: Small Portrait Studies,* Marlborough Fine Art, London, 1993

Michael Peppiatt, *Francis Bacon: Anatomy of an Enigma*, London, 1996

France Borel, with an introduction by Milan Kundera, *Bacon: Portraits and Self-portraits*, London, 1997

David Sylvester, *Looking Back at Francis Bacon*, London, 2000

Grey Gowrie, Louis le Brocquy, Anthony Cronin, Paul Durcan and David Sylvester (with an introduction by Barbara Dawson), *Francis Bacon in Dublin*, Hugh Lane Municipal Gallery of Modern Art, Dublin, 2000

Barbara Dawson and Margarita Cappock, *Francis Bacon's Studio at the Hugh Lane*, Hugh Lane Municipal Gallery of Modern Art, Dublin, 2001

Colm Tóibín, 'Francis Bacon: The Art of Looking', in *Love in a Dark Time and Other Explorations of Gay Lives and Literature*, New York, 2001

Wilfred Seipel, Barbara Steffen and Christoph Vitali (eds.), *Francis Bacon and the Tradition of Art*, Kunsthistorisches Museum, Vienna / Fondation Beyeler, Riehen-Basel, 2003

Martin Harrison, *In Camera. Francis Bacon: Photography, Film and the Practice of Painting*, London, 2005

Martin Hammer, *Bacon and Sutherland*, New Haven and London, 2005

RELATED LITERATURE

Jonathan Dollimore, *Death, Desire and Loss in Western Culture*, London, 1998, especially the chapters on Nietzsche and Bataille

Florian Ebner, *Metamorphosen des Gesichts: Die 'Verwandlungen durch Licht' von Helmar Lerski*, Museum Folkwang Essen/Steidl Verlag, 2002

Monika Faber and Janos Frecot (ed.), *Portraits of an Age: Photography in Germany and Austria 1900–1938*, Neue Galerie, New York; Albertina, Vienna / Hatje Cantz Verlag, 2005

Published by the Trustees of the National Galleries of Scotland
in association with the British Council to accompany the
exhibition *Francis Bacon: Portraits and Heads* held at the
Scottish National Gallery of Modern Art, Edinburgh, from 4 June
until 4 September 2005 and at the Hamburg Kunsthalle from
13 October 2005 until 15 January 2006.

The exhibition is a collaboration between the Scottish National
Gallery of Modern Art and the British Council, in association with
the Hamburg Kunsthalle.

ISBN 1 903278 66 X

Catalogue designed and typeset in Arnhem Blond by Dalrymple
Printed in Poland, OZGraf SA

Front cover: detail from Francis Bacon
Study for Head of George Dyer, 1967 (30)
Private collection

Back cover: Unknown photographer *Francis Bacon*
Dublin City Gallery The Hugh Lane

Frontispiece: *Francis Bacon, strip of passport photographs*
Dublin City Gallery The Hugh Lane

PHOTOGRAPHIC CREDITS

© ADAGP, Paris and DACS, London 2005 figs.3,4; Per Anders Allsten 43;
Jörg P. Anders 51; Francis Bacon studio material © The Estate of Francis
Bacon / Dublin City Art Gallery The Hugh Lane; Richard Caspole 5;
Marlene Burston 46; Prudence Cuming Associates Ltd 16, 18, 37;
Walter Klein 13; RMN–CNAC/MNAM Phillippe Migeat 36; RMN–Bertrand
Prévost 53; Antonia Reeve 6, 19, 26, 27, page 92; R. Schalchi, Zurich 41;
© Tate, London fig.1; Rodney Todd-White 45; Jan Uvelius 25;
Malcolm Varon–NY 38.

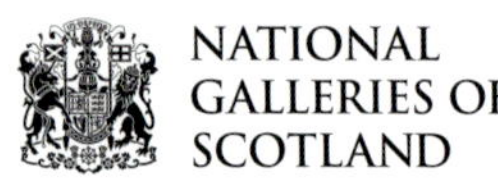
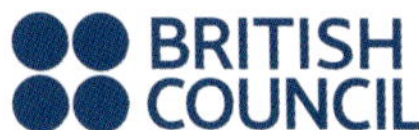